UWEM ESSIA

FISCAL POLITICS INTRIGUES: MANAGING COVID-19 CRISIS AND BUDGET SCRUTINY STRATEGIES

Using Fiscal Policy to Tame Inflation and Protect the Most Vulnerable

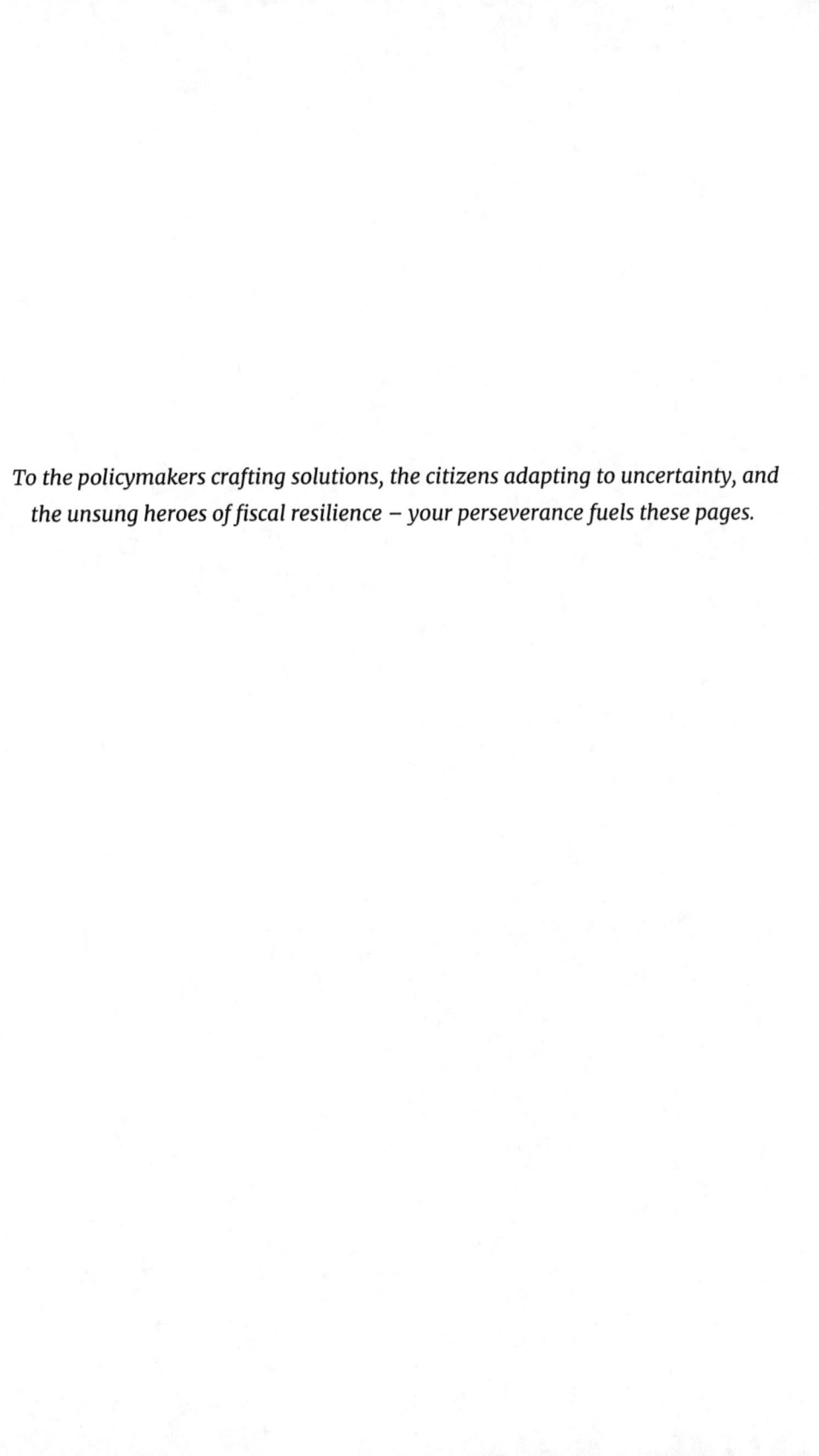

To the policymakers crafting solutions, the citizens adapting to uncertainty, and the unsung heroes of fiscal resilience – your perseverance fuels these pages.

Contents

Preface

The book "Fiscal Politics Intrigues," delves into the intricacies of fiscal decision-making, crisis response, and the critical role of budget scrutiny in navigating the challenges posed by the COVID-19 pandemic. Chapter One initiates the journey by tracing the historical evolution of fiscal policy. From the formative stages, where fiscal policies were loosely defined, to the transformative impact of Keynes' General Theory, the chapter emphasizes the pivotal role of governments in shaping economic paths. The exploration extends to contemporary challenges, unraveling complexities in taxing digital transactions, addressing Base Erosion and Profit Shifting (BEPS), and embracing sustainability through green fiscal policies.

Chapter Two unfolds the canvas of economic policy in action, highlighting the collaboration between the government's fiscal policy and the Federal Reserve's monetary policy. It sheds light on governments' tools to stimulate or cool down economies, emphasizing the impact on income distribution and resource allocation. The chapter culminates in a comprehensive analysis of the fiscal response to the 2007-2008 Great Recession, underlining the importance of timely, targeted, and temporary measures.

Chapter Three confronts the dual challenges of health and economic crises triggered by the unprecedented COVID-19 pandemic. It meticulously navigates through the four phases of policy response, dissecting the tax policies implemented across various countries. The chapter offers a panoramic view of the multifaceted responses to the crisis, from strategies supporting businesses and households to measures boosting investment and consumption.

Chapter Four further delves into tax policies and resilience-building strategies for a speedy recovery from the pandemic. The chapter examines the anticipated global impact on tax revenues, budget balances, and public debts by addressing liquidity management, social protection systems, tax administration efficiency, and stimulus measures. It accentuates the importance of domestic resource mobilization through effective taxation, including property and carbon taxes.

Chapter Five takes us into the Euro Area, navigating the challenges of high inflation and external shocks. The chapter dissects the intricate relationship between inflation and public finances, scrutinizes fiscal policy responses, and assesses the automatic adjustments to cope with high inflation. The distributional impact of fiscal measures is scrutinized, revealing disparities in the purchasing power of different income groups.

Chapter Six explores the nexus of inflation management, fiscal politics, and tax treaties. It unveils the distributive effects of unexpected inflation, assesses its impact on households, and underscores the crucial role of fiscal policy in managing inflation. The chapter explores growth channels, equity implications of fiscal reforms, and the inherent political dynamics that shape fiscal policymaking.

Chapter Seven introduces the concept of Implementation Analysis, providing a structured framework for anticipating and addressing implementation issues in government programs. From the scope and challenges to the benefits and compliance challenges, the chapter offers insights into ensuring better government performance through sustained attention and standardized methodologies.

Chapter Eight concludes our exploration by scrutinizing fiscal councils and independent budget offices. Through case studies from Belgium to the United States, the chapter unravels these institutions' evolution, challenges, and successes, offering lessons for emerging fiscal councils worldwide.

As we embark on this enlightening journey through "FISCAL POLITICS INTRIGUES," we invite readers to immerse themselves in the complexities and nuances of fiscal decision-making, crisis management, and budget scrutiny. May the insights shared within these chapters contribute to a deeper understanding of the challenges and strategies that shape our fast-changing government policy landscape.

INTRODUCTION

In today's complex interplay of economics, politics, and governance, fiscal policies are the bedrock upon which nations build their economic destinies. This book explores the intricate landscape of fiscal decision-making, crisis management, and the critical scrutiny of budgets in an evolving global stage defined by the unprecedented challenges posed by the 2008 Great Recession and the recent COVID-19 pandemic. Within this crucible of change and adaptation, "FISCAL POLITICS INTRIGUES" unfolds, inviting readers on a compelling journey through the corridors of fiscal intricacies and global crisis management strategies.

Our exploration commences with Chapter One: Fiscal Policy: From Historical Evolution to Contemporary Challenges, where the historical evolution of fiscal policy is unveiled. From the loosely defined fiscal policies of the pre-Keynesian era to the transformative impact of Keynes' General Theory, the chapter underscores the pivotal role governments play in shaping economic paths. It dissects contemporary challenges, addresses the complexities of taxing digital transactions, contends with Base Erosion and Profit Shifting (BEPS), and embraces innovative sustainability through green fiscal policies.

As we turn the pages to Chapter Two: Economic Policy in Action, the collaborative dance between fiscal and monetary policies takes centre stage. Distinctions between these policies are delineated, illuminating the intricate collaboration between the executive and legislative branches in the United States. The chapter unveils the tools governments employ to stimulate or cool down economies, emphasizing their varied impacts on income distribution and resource allocation. The narrative crescendos with a detailed analysis of the response to the 2007-2008 Great Recession, emphasizing the indispensable qualities of timely, targeted, and temporary measures.

Chapter Three, Tax Policy Responses to the Dual Challenges of Health and Economic Crisis, propels us to the heart of the challenges posed by the COVID-19 pandemic. This chapter unfolds the four phases of policy response, providing a comprehensive review of tax measures across nations. This chapter paints a vivid panorama of global responses to the crisis, from strategies supporting businesses and households to diverse measures boosting investment and consumption.

The canvas broadens in Chapter Four: Tax Policies and Resilience-Building for Speedy Recovery from the COVID-19 Pandemic. Strategies for liquidity management, the role of social protection systems, tax administration efficiency, and the design principles for effective stimulus packages come to the fore. The chapter meticulously analyzes the anticipated global impact on tax revenues, budget balances, and public debts, emphasizing the need for innovative financing approaches and effective domestic resource mobilization through taxation.

Chapter Five: Fiscal Policy Challenges in the Euro Area transports us to the Eurozone, where the rising spectra of high inflation and external shocks profoundly impact. From unravelling inflation dynamics to scrutinizing fiscal policy responses and their distributional impacts, this chapter lays bare the intricacies of managing economic stability in the face of formidable challenges.

Chapter Six: Inflation Management, Fiscal Politics and Tax Treaties delve into the profound implications of inflation on debt dynamics, its impact on households, and the vital role of fiscal policy in managing inflation. The chapter explores growth channels, the equity implications of fiscal reforms, and the inherently political nature of fiscal policymaking.

The journey through fiscal intricacies and crisis management strategies takes an insightful turn in Chapter Seven: Meaning and Application of Implementation Analysis. This chapter introduces the concept of Implementation Analysis, offering a structured framework to anticipate and address implementation issues in government programs. It underscores the need for sustained attention and standardized methodologies to ensure better government performance and achieve policy objectives.

Our odyssey concludes with Chapter Eight: Fiscal Scrutiny, where we scrutinize case studies of fiscal councils and independent budget offices. From Belgium to the United States, these case studies unravel the evolution, challenges, and successes of institutions tasked with fiscal scrutiny, providing invaluable lessons for emerging fiscal councils worldwide.

As we embark on this intellectual voyage through "FISCAL POLITICS INTRIGUES," we invite readers to immerse themselves in the complexities and nuances of fiscal decision-making, crisis management, and the critical scrutiny of budgets, hoping that the insights shared within these chapters contribute to a deeper understanding of the challenges and strategies that shape our economic landscape.

CHAPTER ONE: FISCAL POLICY: FROM HISTORICAL EVOLUTION TO CONTEMPORARY CHALLENGES

Summary of Key Points

1. Government's Crucial Role: Government plays a pivotal role in shaping economic paths through fiscal policies involving Taxation, expenditure, and national budgets. Societal principles, behavioral economics, and market failures justify government intervention.

2. Public Goods and Market Failure: Public goods, non-excludable and non-rivalrous, require government intervention due to market failures. Social goods, a subset, are provided for societal benefit. Market failures arise from the unique nature of public goods, necessitating government involvement.

3. Evolution of Fiscal Policy: The pre-Keynesian era had a loosely defined fiscal policy, evolving through debates like the British tariff debates. Keynes' General Theory in 1936 marked a significant shift, contributing to the rise of Macroeconomics and modern Public Economics.

4. Contemporary Fiscal Challenges: Taxing digital transactions faces complexities due to global operations and intangible assets. Base Erosion and Profit Shifting (BEPS) by companies exploiting tax rules pose challenges to the tax base in countries.

5. Global Initiatives: OECD/G20 aims to establish new regulations for profit

allocation in the digital economy. Some countries implement Digital Services Taxes (DST), but a globally coordinated solution is essential to avoid trade tensions.

6. Sustainability and Green Fiscal Policies: Environmental Taxation, incentives for sustainable practices, and contemporary challenges in the digital economy require innovative solutions. Governments are adopting carbon pricing and providing incentives for green investments.

Fiscal policy plays a crucial role in shaping the economic path of any nation through two key governmental activities: Taxation (including subsidies) and expenditure. The national budget is the primary fiscal tool, allowing the government to determine how resources are allocated between these vital functions. Why is government essential? Why not entrust the entire economic landscape to market dynamics? The answer lies in widely accepted societal principles, such as aligning output with individual consumer preferences and advocating for decentralized decision-making. Furthermore, deviations from consumer choice and decentralized decisions rooted in political and social ideologies justify the need for government presence. Equally important is the behavioral economics view that individuals do not always act in their best interest.

The public sector needs to step in to regulate and rectify certain aspects of private sector activities, making the involvement of government in the economy a necessary technical consideration rather than an ideological choice. More precisely, government intervention is imperative in economic activities for various reasons:

1. Efficient Resource Use: Government regulation must ensure free entry and full market knowledge for competitive factors and product markets.
2. Inefficiencies in Competition: Public sector involvement becomes essential when competition is inefficient due to decreasing costs.
3. Legal Infrastructure: The market relies on government-provided legal structures to safeguard contractual arrangements and exchanges.

4. Externalities and Market Failure: Public sector solutions are required when goods face market exclusion due to "externalities" and "market failure."

5. Social Values and Income Distribution: Income and wealth distribution adjustments, influenced by social values and market-driven property rights transmission, may require public intervention.

6. Economic Objectives: Public policy is crucial for achieving high employment, price stability, and desired economic growth rates in advanced financial economies.

7. Differing Valuation Perspectives: The discount rate for valuing future consumption may vary between public and private viewpoints.

Indeed, it may be correct to argue that an economy may not be said to exist in the real sense where there is no government.

A Focus on Taxation and Fiscal Policy

While recognizing the limitations of the market mechanism and the need for corrective public policy measures, it is crucial to acknowledge that not all policy interventions guarantee improved economic system performance. Like private policy, public policy is often subject to inefficiencies for several reasons, including inadequate data to arrive at the correct judgment and that sometimes, good economics could be better politics. Our study of fiscal policy aims to understand how the formulation and application of policies can be enhanced for optimal effectiveness.

Public Goods and Market Failure

In economic terms, a public good is characterized by being both non-excludable and non-rivalrous, meaning individuals cannot be effectively excluded from consuming it, and one person's use does not diminish its availability to others. Public goods, such as fresh air, national security, and street lighting, serve the collective benefit. Public goods often face challenges such as excessive use leading to negative externalities, exemplified by air pollution. Technological progress can introduce new public goods, like official statistics, advancing decision-making capabilities. The opposite of public goods is private goods, like a loaf of bread, which can be excluded from use by others. Goods that are rivalrous but non-excludable are termed common-pool resources.

Social Goods: Social goods, a subset of public goods, are typically delivered by the government for various reasons, including social policy. Examples include clean air, clean water, and literacy. Understanding these distinctions is vital for formulating effective policies that cater to the diverse needs of society.

Market Failure in Providing Public and Social Goods: The fundamental reason behind market failure in delivering public and social goods lies in the unique nature of the benefits these goods generate. Unlike private goods, where benefits are confined to consumer purchasing, public and social goods offer benefits that extend to others. This characteristic leads to market failure, where individual gain-seeking behavior fails to yield efficient outcomes. Applying the exclusion principle—excluding consumers unless they pay— is an efficient solution with private goods. However, this is impossible with public and social goods due to their unique characteristics. Exclusion becomes inefficient when consumers' participation does not diminish others' consumption. The market mechanism falters in the absence of benefits being vested in property rights. Government intervention becomes necessary to address market failures and ensure equitable provision when benefits are universally available, leading to a severed link between producer and consumer."

Government's Role in Public Goods Provision: The government provides public goods since the private sector must be more efficiently equipped for this task. However, challenges arise in determining these goods' quantity, quality, type, and pricing. Societal preferences, needs, and the political process are crucial in making these determinations, but optimal results are only sometimes achieved.

Free-Riding and Government Intervention: Individual consumers need more incentives to voluntarily disclose how they value public services to the government, leading to an ineffective voluntary tax system. People prefer to benefit as "free riders" from others' contributions. The political process is a substitute for the market mechanism to address this challenge. The difficulty lies in accurately valuing these benefits, requiring innovative techniques to determine the supply of public goods and allocate costs effectively.

Differentiating Public Provision and Production: Provisioning and production are distinguishable in economics. The government can concession the production and or provisioning of a public or publicized good to the private sector.

Evolution of Fiscal Policy

Pre-Keynesian Era

The period before 1936 witnessed a diverse and loosely defined concept of fiscal policy, encompassing various topics such as taxes, international trade policy, and public debt financing. Fiscal policy was perceived as rudimentary and idiosyncratic, reflecting a responsive approach to external pressures, including political dynamics and public sentiment regarding the role of economics in shaping the government's actions. The professionalization of economics in the late 19th century, marked by the establishment of academic organizations and journals, contributed to a more controlled and deliberate use of terminology. By 1900, the term "fiscal policy" was associated with tariff policy, tax policy, and government debt financing. In summary, the pre-Keynesian era showcased a dynamically evolving concept of fiscal policy, reflecting changing perceptions of the government's role in the economy. Understanding this evolution is crucial for comprehending the rise of macroeconomics and the development of modern public economics.

British Tariff Debates (1900-1905) A significant moment for fiscal policy unfolded during the British tariff debates initiated by Joseph Chamberlain at the turn of the 20th century. Motivated partly by severe recessions in Great Britain, protectionism emerged as a strategy to alleviate unemployment and boost domestic manufacturing. Chamberlain's "Imperial Fiscal Policy" proposed preferential tariffs for British colonies and import duties for others, departing significantly from Britain's historical free trade stance. Advocates argued that this fiscal policy would protect British industries suffering under laissez-faire policies adopted by the United States, France, and Germany in the preceding decade.

Between 1901 and 1905, the term "fiscal policy(ies)" appeared 1,849 times in The Times (London), reflecting the heightened discourse during this era. Economists, including members of the German Historical School, explored whether fiscal policy could be employed to influence national employment outcomes. Despite Chamberlain's considerable support in the popular press, economists, leveraging their professional positions, signed "The Manifesto for Free Trade" in 1903, opposing government intervention in trade. Notable economists like Alfred Marshall and J.A. Hobson provided analyses refuting Chamberlain's proposals, emphasizing the impracticality of a scientific fiscal policy. Despite Chamberlain's electoral defeat in 1906, proposals linking governmental action, or fiscal policy, to deliberately shaping national economic outcomes continued. For instance, "A Fiscal Policy for Labor" suggested income and inheritance tax reforms to benefit the laboring classes and enhance employment.

The evolution of Macroeconomics and the incorporation of fiscal policy as a vital tool originated in the 20th century, marking a significant shift from Public Finance. John Maynard Keynes' groundbreaking work, "The General Theory of Employment, Interest, and Money" (1936), is pivotal in understanding the historical trajectory of fiscal policy. By formulating "a theory of output as a whole," Keynes laid the foundation for Macroeconomics, intertwining unemployment, wages, taxes, business cycles, interest, output, and money. His work redefined fiscal policy, giving it a new perspective and meaning in the context of government finance. "fiscal policy" was not explicitly defined in "The General Theory." However, the book provided the theoretical basis for understanding its profound impact on the national economy. Keynes rightly contributed to introducing and popularizing the term in modern economic discourse.

Politics and Fiscal Policy (1900-1920)

From 1900 to 1920, the application and interpretation of fiscal policy experienced notable fluctuations influenced by concurrent political events. The term "new fiscal policy" had emerged as early as the 1870s, signifying protectionist trade measures in response to economic, particularly agricultural, fluctuations. The period from 1900 to 1920 saw a close connection between fiscal policy and three distinct political-economic discussions: the British tariff debates on national trade policy, the role of fiscal policy as tax policy in the push for a federal income tax in the United States, and the link between fiscal policy and public debt financing during the First World War.

The U.S. Income Tax: In the subsequent decade, tariffs remained both a revenue source and a mechanism for industry protection, often under the umbrella term "fiscal policy." However, not everyone welcomed this broad application of the term. Cohn (1904, 194) argued that referring to the Zollpolitik (tariff politics) of Germany as "fiscal policy" lacked clarity since "fiscal" pertains to levies for revenue, not for commercial policy. This viewpoint gained traction as "fiscal policy" transitioned from trade literature to public finance, primarily driven by the movement for a progressive national income tax in the United States.

Before 1914, the U.S. federal government relied on tariffs, duties, stamp taxes, and property taxes for revenue. The general property tax, a foundation of American fiscal policy, faced criticism for its antiquated and inequitable structure. The debate over implementing a national income tax intensified, dominating discussions in economics journals and major newspapers. Articles on taxation issues constituted the majority of references to "fiscal policy(ies)" in economics journals and the New York Times during this period.

American Progressive economists advocating for a national income tax drew inspiration from fiscal reforms in continental Europe. Influenced by the German model of professional economists trained by universities and employed by the government, they envisioned a role for economists in managing the economy. The passage of the Sixteenth Amendment marked a shift from debating the necessity of an income tax to discussing its management and the budget. The emergence of the "science" of budget management emphasized the executive nature of fiscal policy. Experts emphasized the need for a harmonious program correlating various aspects of a proper fiscal policy, considering specific outcomes such as reducing income inequality and increasing employment.

Unlike wartime measures that imposed temporary demands on national finances, the national income tax gave economists a permanent advisory role in government, allowing for tax policies to achieve economic, political, and social objectives. Although delayed by the First World War, the national income tax paved the way for utilizing tax measures to accomplish broader social goals, demonstrating that "fiscal policy" could serve as a tool to engineer diverse national economic outcomes.

The Evolution of Fiscal Policy: From Pre-War Dynamics to the Great Depression

The First World War – Shifting Dynamics of Fiscal Policy: The imperative need to finance great wars significantly altered perspectives on fiscal policy, covering tax policy, tariff policy, industrial/commercial policy, and public debt. By 1916, the realization that the war would be prolonged and costly intensified economists' focus on war finance. More scholars used the term "fiscal policy(ies)" to address war finance or debt. While public finance primarily addressed war funding concerning fiscal policy, the term retained its eclectic usage. The "scientific fiscal policy" concept gained prominence, emphasizing systematic cooperation between all productive forces, assuming common aims between government and people. A.C. Pigou laid the theoretical groundwork, advocating for expanded government management through fiscal policy to increase national income, distribute wealth more equally, and reduce economic fluctuations. Pigou suggested state regulation of public services and works to stabilize the economy during recessions.

Interwar Years - Fiscal Policy in Transition: In the 1920s, economists continued using the term "fiscal policy" with war debts in focus. Concerns about war debts increased. The post-World War I discussions on public debt integrated Taxation and monetary economics, with public debt management becoming crucial in public finance. During the interwar, fiscal policies were increasingly associated with economic fluctuations, unemployment, and national income. Business cycle theory, emerging post-World War I, gained prominence. The National Bureau of Economic Research (NBER) was founded in 1920, focusing on the statistical analysis of business cycles. Economists explored "fiscal policy" in the context of managing economic uncertainties. The popular press continued to use the fiscal policy to cover Taxation, debt, trade, cycles, and unemployment. Governments, facing post-war challenges, expressed the need for a "general fiscal policy" to stimulate manufacturing and exports.

Fiscal Policy and the Great Depression - An Era of Transformation: Political events, the rise of professional economists, and evolving views on the economic role of government paved the way for diverse interpretations of fiscal policy by the late 1920s. The stock market crash 1929 and the subsequent Great Depression compelled economists to view fiscal policy as a potential tool for economic management. The dominant academic discourse focused on aspects of the depression, revealing divergent views on fiscal policy. Public debt, inflation, deflation, and currency management. Became the leading topic in the first fiscal policy course introduced by Henry Simons at the University of Chicago in 1934. In the run-up to Keynes' General Theory in 1936, the concept of "fiscal policy" shifted from a mere means of raising government funds to a tool for engineering national economic outcomes. The prolonged depression forced economists to explore whether fiscal policies could achieve specific macroeconomic objectives. The period they marked a significant transition, laying the groundwork for the Keynesian revolution in the 1940s and 1950s.

Navigating Contemporary Challenges in Public Finance

Addressing contemporary issues in public finance, especially in the digital economy and sustainability, demands innovative solutions. Challenges in taxing digital transactions and implementing green fiscal policies underscore the need for dynamic approaches. Some of the contemporary challenges in public finance are summarized below:

Challenges in Taxing Digital Transactions

Taxing digital transactions involves intricacies tied to global operations and intangible assets, challenging traditional tax systems based on physical presence. Determining the appropriate jurisdiction for taxing digital transactions becomes a complex task, given the borderless nature of digital businesses. Global Nature of Transactions: Digital businesses operating globally challenge traditional tax systems rooted in physical presence, leading to difficulties in determining the appropriate jurisdiction for taxing digital transactions.

The intangibility of Assets: The intangibility of digital goods and services poses valuation and taxation challenges in areas like digital advertising, cloud computing, and online marketplaces. Example: Tech giants like Amazon, Google, and Facebook have faced scrutiny for minimizing tax liabilities, sparking debates about the fairness and adequacy of existing tax frameworks.

Base Erosion and Profit Shifting (BEPS): Companies exploit gaps in tax rules, shifting profits to low-tax locations, leading to erosion of the tax base in other countries. Tech giants like Amazon, Google, and Facebook face scrutiny for minimizing tax liabilities, raising concerns about the fairness of existing tax frameworks."

Global Initiatives in Addressing Taxation Challenges

1. OECD/G20 Inclusive Framework: The collaborative endeavors of OECD and G20 countries are directed towards establishing new regulations for profit allocation, ensuring an equitable distribution of Taxation in the digital economy.

2. Digital Services Taxes (DST): Certain countries are unilaterally implementing Digital Services Taxes (DSTs) to tax the revenues of major digital companies. However, this approach leads to trade tensions, underscoring the imperative for a globally coordinated solution. Example: The United Kingdom, France, and Italy have introduced or proposed DSTs to tax large digital companies' revenues. However, unilateral measures have sparked trade tensions, prompting calls for a coordinated global solution.

3. Sustainability and Green Fiscal Policies: Environmental Taxation: Governments are adopting carbon pricing mechanisms and levies on single-use plastics to internalize external costs and tackle environmental concerns.

4. Incentives for Sustainable Practices: Green subsidies and tax credits are being employed to incentivize industries and individuals to adopt environmentally friendly practices, facilitating the transition to cleaner energy sources.

5. Future Trends and Challenges: Technological Innovations and Public Finance: Blockchain and smart contracts can transform fiscal processes by enhancing transparency and reducing reliance on intermediaries.

6. Artificial Intelligence in Predictive Analytics: Artificial intelligence aids in predictive analytics, offering valuable insights into economic trends, tax compliance, and revenue patterns.

7. Demographic Shifts and Fiscal Implications: Aging populations present challenges to pension systems, necessitating reforms such as adjustments to retirement age and contribution rates. Demographic shifts result in higher healthcare expenditures, requiring preventive measures and technological investments to manage costs effectively.

Sustainability and Green Fiscal Policies

Environmental Taxation: a. Carbon Pricing: Governments adopt carbon pricing mechanisms like carbon taxes or cap-and-trade systems to internalize external costs, incentivizing businesses to reduce carbon emissions. b. Plastic Taxes: Some countries impose taxes on single-use plastics to discourage their use and address environmental concerns. Example: Sweden's carbon tax, initiated in the early 1990s, has successfully incentivized industries to reduce carbon emissions, with tax revenue funding renewable energy projects.

Incentives for Sustainable Practices: a. Green Subsidies: Governments provide subsidies to industries engaged in sustainable practices, such as renewable energy production. b. Tax Credits for Green Investments: Tax incentives are offered for environmentally friendly activities, including investments in renewable energy, energy-efficient buildings, and electric vehicles. Example: The U.S. Investment Tax Credit (ITC) and Production Tax Credit (PTC) provide incentives for investments in renewable energy projects, promoting the transition to cleaner energy sources.

Contemporary issues in public finance, especially in the digital economy and sustainability, pose unique challenges. Taxing digital transactions involves complexities, while green fiscal policies are crucial in aligning economic activities with environmental goals. Real-world examples demonstrate ongoing efforts to balance economic growth with fair and sustainable fiscal policies.

Technological Innovations and Public Finance

Blockchain and Smart Contracts: Blockchain technology and smart contracts disrupt traditional banking systems through decentralized finance (DeFi). Smart contracts automate contractual agreements on blockchain platforms, potentially reducing the need for intermediaries. Example: In public finance, blockchain could revolutionize government procurement processes. Smart contracts enhance transparency and efficiency in contract execution, automating tasks and reducing the risk of fraud.

Artificial Intelligence in Fiscal Planning: Artificial Intelligence (AI) in predictive analytics analyzes vast data sets to accurately predict economic trends, tax evasion risks, and revenue patterns. AI tools improve tax compliance by identifying irregularities and potential tax evasion, strengthening fiscal planning and revenue collection. Example: Singapore's Inland Revenue Authority utilizes AI to enhance tax compliance. Machine learning algorithms analyze taxpayer data to identify patterns and assess compliance risks, contributing to effective fiscal planning.

Demographic Shifts and Fiscal Implications: Aging Populations and Pension Systems: Aging populations increase demand for pension payments, challenging pension systems. Governments may implement reforms to ensure sustainability, such as raising the retirement age or adjusting contribution rates. Example: Japan addresses challenges with an aging population through pension reforms, including changes in eligibility age and encouragement of private pension plans.

Impact on Healthcare Expenditures: Demographic shifts, like an aging population, lead to higher healthcare costs. Governments focus on preventive healthcare measures and technology investments to manage healthcare budgets efficiently. Example: European countries, such as Germany, implement healthcare reforms to address challenges from an aging population. These reforms aim to improve healthcare delivery efficiency and contain costs.

In summary, future trends and challenges in public finance hinge on technological innovations and demographic shifts. Blockchain and AI present transformative opportunities, enhancing transparency and efficiency. Demographic shifts require thoughtful policy reforms in pension and healthcare systems. Governments must proactively adapt to these trends, leveraging technology and implementing policy reforms for sustainable and efficient public finance systems. Real-world examples illustrate ongoing efforts in response to these trends."

Contemporary Use of the Term "Fiscal Policy"

In contemporary use, fiscal policy refers to the government's spending and tax policies influencing macroeconomic conditions, such as aggregate demand, employment, inflation, and economic growth. In times of recession, the government may lower taxes or increase spending to stimulate demand and economic activity. Conversely, during periods of inflation, it may raise taxes or cut spending to cool down the economy. Fiscal policy differs from monetary policy, which is managed by central bankers rather than elected government officials.

The foundation of U.S. fiscal policy draws heavily from Keynes's argument that economic recessions result from consumer spending and business investment deficiencies. The New Deal in the U.S., a response to the Great Depression, implemented massive spending on public works projects and social welfare programs based on Keynesian principles. Keynesian economists argue that private sector components of aggregate demand are too variable and emotionally driven to sustain economic growth. Pessimism and fear can lead to recessions, while excessive optimism can result in an overheated economy. According to Keynesians, governments can manage Taxation and spending more rationally to stabilize the economy.

Corrective Government Fiscal Action: To counteract private sector deficiencies, the government can increase spending or reduce taxes during economic downturns, known as expansionary fiscal policies. Conversely, during economic upswings, the government can reduce spending or raise taxes, termed contractionary fiscal policies. These actions aim to stabilize the economy, with large budget deficits during downturns and surpluses during growth periods. Accordingly, in a recession, the government may issue tax stimulus rebates or increase spending to boost aggregate demand, fueling economic growth. This approach, characterized by deficit spending, creates a positive feedback loop, lowering unemployment and increasing consumer income. However, to counter inflation, the government may pursue contractionary fiscal policy involving tax increases, reduced public spending, and job cuts. This strategy, associated with budget surpluses, is used less frequently due to political unpopularity.

Critics argue that expansionary fiscal policies, resulting in mounting deficits, can negatively impact economic growth and necessitate damaging austerity measures. Some economists contend that increased government spending may crowd out private-sector investment. It is essential to note that expansionary policies can be politically challenging to reverse, leading to continuous deficit spending and potentially causing economic imbalances. Governments should carefully manage these policies to avoid risks such as inflation and asset bubbles that could harm the economy.

Review Questions

1. Why is government intervention crucial in ensuring efficient resource use and competition in the market?
2. What were the key debates and shifts in fiscal policy during the pre-Keynesian era, especially during the British tariff debates?
3. How does the unique nature of public goods lead to market failures, and why is government intervention necessary in such cases?
4. What are the challenges in taxing digital transactions, and how are global initiatives addressing these challenges?
5. Explain the role of fiscal policies during the Great Depression and how it led to the Keynesian revolution.
6. What are the contemporary issues in public finance related to sustainability, and how are governments addressing them through fiscal policies?

Discussion Points

1. Balancing Act: Discuss the delicate balance governments must strike in implementing fiscal policies to stimulate economic growth without leading to detrimental consequences like inflation or deficits.
2. Global Collaboration: Explore the challenges and benefits of global collaboration in addressing fiscal issues, especially in the context of

digital transactions and environmental policies.

3. Technological Integration: Discuss the impact of technological innovations like blockchain and AI on fiscal processes, considering opportunities and challenges.

CHAPTER TWO: ECONOMIC POLICY IN ACTION: FROM FISCAL RESPONSE TO GLOBAL CRISES

Summary of Key Points

1. Distinctions Between Fiscal and Monetary Policy:

- Fiscal policy, managed by the government, involves taxation and government spending to influence economic activity.
- Monetary policy, overseen by the Federal Reserve, adjusts the money supply to impact liquidity, focusing on interest rates and inflation.

2. Government Collaboration in Fiscal Policy:

- Fiscal policy in the U.S. involves collaboration between the executive and legislative branches, with the President, Secretary of the Treasury, and Congress playing crucial roles.
- The collaboration includes deliberation, approval, and execution of measures to achieve economic goals.

3. Tools of Fiscal Policy:

- Fiscal tools include taxation adjustments and changes in government spending to stimulate or cool down the economy.

- Government decisions on taxation and spending have varied impacts on specific groups, influencing income distribution and resource allocation.

4. Fiscal Policy Objectives:

- Fiscal policy aims for short-term stabilization and long-term goals like sustainable growth and poverty reduction.
- Objectives depend on factors such as the business cycle, natural disasters, and demographic considerations.

5. Response to the 2007-2008 Great Recession:

- The global crisis led to responses through automatic stabilizers and fiscal stimulus to counter consumption, investment, and international trade declines.
- The effectiveness of responses depends on a government's fiscal space and ability to manage deficits and debt ratios.

6. Timing and Nature of Stimulus:

- Timely, targeted, and temporary measures are crucial for effective stimulus.
- The hazard of expansionary policies lies in potential macroeconomic distortions, outdated analysis, and corruption risks.

Fiscal Policy vs. Monetary Policy

Fiscal policy, managed by the government, involves using taxes and government spending to stimulate or slow economic activity. On the other hand, monetary policy is overseen by the U.S. Federal Reserve Board and focuses on adjusting the nation's money supply to increase or decrease liquidity. The Federal Reserve aims to achieve Congress-instructed economic goals such as maximum employment, stable prices, and moderate long-term interest rates. The tools used by the Federal Reserve for monetary policy include buying/selling securities, lending to depository institutions, adjusting the discount rate, managing the federal funds rate, establishing reserve requirements, engaging in central bank liquidity swaps, and financing through overnight repurchase agreements.

In the United States, fiscal policy is a collaboration between the executive and legislative branches. The President and the Secretary of the Treasury in the executive branch play significant roles, often consulting with a Council of Economic Advisers. The U.S. Congress, representing the legislative branch, authorizes taxes, enacts laws, and appropriates spending for fiscal policy measures through its power of the purse, involving participation, deliberation, and approval from the House of Representatives and the Senate.

While monetary and fiscal policies share the goal of influencing the economy, there are fundamental distinctions between the two. The tools employed by each policy also differ significantly. Monetary policy utilizes open market operations, reserve requirements, and the discount rate, while fiscal policy involves government spending adjustments and alterations to tax policies. Through monetary policy, central banks manipulate interest rates and the money supply, impacting inflation and economic growth. Fiscal policy, managed by governments, operates through changes in spending and taxation. Determining the superiority of either policy depends on the specific circumstances and the type of policy enacted. Lowering interest rates via monetary policy makes borrowing cheaper, encouraging consumer debt and business investments. Conversely, fiscal policy boosts gross domestic product (GDP) by increasing demand for goods and services, leading to higher prices and output.

Monetary and fiscal policy share common objectives of stabilizing a country's economy. Their optimal effectiveness often emerges when implemented together. Monetary policy influences financial markets, while fiscal policy directly impacts the money individuals have at their disposal. Both policies play significant roles in managing the economy, exerting direct and indirect effects on personal and household finances. Fiscal policy, involving tax and spending decisions, influences tax bills and employs government projects. Meanwhile, monetary policy, overseen by the central bank, bolsters consumer spending through interest rate adjustments.

Main Tools of Fiscal Policy

Governments use fiscal policy tools to influence the economy, primarily through taxation and government spending changes. To stimulate growth, taxes are lowered, and spending is increased, often involving borrowing through government debt issuance. Conversely, taxes may be raised to cool down an overheating economy, and spending may decrease. However, the effects of fiscal policy are not uniformly experienced. Depending on policymakers' goals, a tax cut may benefit only the middle class during economic declines, while the same group may face higher taxes during economic downturns. Similarly, government spending decisions can impact specific groups, with infrastructure projects benefiting construction workers and specialized projects benefiting specific experts and firms. These policies can be politically challenging to reverse, leading to continuous deficit spending during economic expansions.

Government Involvement in the Economy: A key challenge for policymakers is determining the extent of government involvement in the economy. Over U.S. history, there have been varying degrees of government interference. While some level of involvement is generally accepted as necessary for a healthy economy, policymakers must strike a balance to sustain economic well-being. Governments directly and indirectly affect resource allocation in the economy through fiscal policy. A national income accounting equation illustrates how government actions impact private consumption, private investment, government spending, and net exports.

Fiscal Policy Objectives: Fiscal policy objectives include short-term macroeconomic stabilization and long-term goals like sustainable growth and poverty reduction. Priorities depend on the country's circumstances, responding to the business cycle, natural disasters, global food or fuel price spikes, development levels, demographics, and natural resources.

Fiscal policy is a vital tool government use to maintain a healthy economy, impacting citizens through taxes, spending, and borrowing. Policymakers strive to achieve macroeconomic stability, sustainable growth, and poverty reduction, navigating challenges and finding the right balance between government involvement and economic well-being.

Fiscal Response to the 2007-2008 Great Recession

The global crisis stemming from the 2007 U.S. mortgage market meltdown is an illustrative case for examining fiscal policy. This crisis, impacting economies worldwide, witnessed challenges in the financial sector and a decline in confidence, leading to setbacks in private consumption, investment, and international trade—factors influencing output and GDP. Governments responded through two channels: automatic stabilizers and fiscal stimulus. Automatic stabilizers activate based on changes in tax revenues and expenditure levels, responding to the business cycle. For example, tax revenues decline during a downturn, and social spending increases. Countries with larger stabilizers relied less on discretionary measures during the recent crisis. Unlike discretionary measures, automatic stabilizers do not face implementation lags and automatically withdraw as conditions improve.

Fiscal Ability to Respond: The effectiveness of the response depends on a government's fiscal space—its capacity for new spending or tax cuts. Governments lacking fiscal space may face constraints due to concerns about inflation, foreign exchange reserves, or doubts about wise spending and the ability to reverse stimulus. Severe financing constraints may lead to spending cuts, while high inflation or external deficits can render fiscal stimulus ineffective. The size, timing, composition, and duration of stimulus matter. Policymakers aim to tailor measures to the output gap and consider factors like the multiplier effect, leakages, monetary conditions, and fiscal sustainability. A balanced approach includes measures targeting low-income people, funding capital investments, and providing tax cuts.

Timing, Targeting, and Temporary Nature of Stimulus

Implementing spending measures takes time, and they may outlast their necessity once in place. However, if a prolonged downturn is expected, concerns over lags may be less pressing. Timely, targeted, and temporary measures are crucial for effective stimulus. A progressive tax system linking transfer payments to economic conditions, fiscal rules during boom times, and sunset mechanisms for programs contribute to the responsiveness and scope of stabilizers. Medium-term frameworks assessing revenues, expenditures, assets, liabilities, and risks improve policymaking over the business cycle.

Big Deficits and Rising Public Debt: Fiscal deficits and public debt ratios (debt-to-GDP ratios) have surged in numerous countries due to the crisis's impact on GDP, tax revenues, and fiscal response costs. Support and guarantees to financial and industrial sectors have raised concerns about governments' financial health. While some countries can manage moderate fiscal deficits, prolonged and excessive deficits may erode confidence. Recognizing these risks, the IMF urged a four-pronged fiscal policy strategy in 2008-2009:

1. Stimulus with no permanent impact on deficits
2. Commitment to fiscal correction in medium-term frameworks
3. Identification and implementation of structural reforms for growth
4. Clear strategies for health care and pension reform in countries facing demographic pressures

This strategy remains pertinent as fiscal challenges persist, especially in advanced economies. Automatic stabilizers are passive, operating without further congressional action, while discretionary fiscal policy is active, using measures to speed up or slow down the economy.

Expansionary fiscal policy occurs when Congress cuts tax rates or increases government spending, shifting aggregate demand right. Contractionary fiscal policy happens when Congress raises tax rates or reduces government spending, shifting aggregate demand left. Policy responses take some time and may not align perfectly, leading to recessions or inflationary pressures.

Business cycles result from aggregate supply and demand shifts, prompting governments to use fiscal policy to address disparities.

Expansionary fiscal policy aims to increase aggregate demand through either heightened government spending or reduced taxes. This policy seeks to:

1. Increase Consumption: By elevating disposable income through personal income tax or payroll tax cuts.
2. Boost Investments: By raising after-tax profits through business tax cuts.
3. Raise Government Purchases: Increasing federal spending on goods and services and grants to state and local governments to enhance their expenditures.

The contractionary fiscal policy operates inversely, aiming to decrease aggregate demand by reducing consumption, investments, and government spending, which can be achieved through spending cuts or tax increases. The appropriateness of expansionary or contractionary fiscal policy can be evaluated using the aggregate demand/supply model. Expansionary fiscal policy can increase aggregate demand, moving the economy to a new equilibrium closer to full employment and potentially causing a minor increase in the price level. The important question is, "Should the government use tax cuts, spending increases, or a combination for expansionary fiscal policy?" After the 2008–2009 recession, the U.S. experienced a substantial budget deficit due to automatic stabilizers and discretionary fiscal policy. While concerns about persistent deficits exist, most economists support larger deficits in the short run during severe recessions.

Politics of Expansionary Fiscal Policy - Tax Cuts vs. Spending Increases: The choice between tax cuts and spending increases often reflects political preferences. Generally, conservatives favor expansionary fiscal policy through tax cuts, while liberals prefer spending increases. For instance, the Obama administration implemented an $830 billion expansionary policy in 2009, involving tax cuts and increased government spending. However, facing budget challenges, state and local governments offset federal expansionary policy by cutting spending. The political debate on policy tools frustrates attempts to label economics as solely liberal or conservative.

Contractionary Fiscal Policy: Curbing an Overheating Economy: Fiscal policy can be employed to counter an overheating economy where the macro equilibrium exceeds potential GDP; in such a scenario, contractionary fiscal policy, involving federal spending cuts or tax increases, can alleviate upward pressure on the price level, by reducing aggregate demand to align with potentially reduced GDP. The conventional macroeconomic model does not prescribe a specific method of implementing contractionary fiscal policy. Preferences may vary, with some favoring spending cuts, others preferring tax increases, and some suggesting context-specific decisions. The model emphasizes the necessity of reducing aggregate demand in this situation.

Automatic Stabilizers: Managing Economic Fluctuations: Automatic stabilizers are tax and spending rules designed to slow the rate of aggregate demand decrease during an economic slowdown and restrain aggregate demand during economic upturns. Unlike discretionary fiscal policy, these stabilizers operate without additional legislative changes.

Expansionary Policy - A Tool for Economic Growth

Expansionary policy utilizes either monetary or fiscal policy, or a combination of both, to address deficiencies in aggregate demand. The objective is to boost business investment and consumer spending by injecting money into the economy. Governments implement expansionary fiscal policy through budgeting tools, injecting money into the economy. Measures include:

1. Increasing Spending: Funding infrastructure projects and social programs.
2. Cutting Taxes: Leaving more money in the hands of consumers to stimulate spending.
3. Transfer Payments: Increasing welfare, unemployment, or other bene-

fits to augment household income.

Expansionary fiscal policy involves direct government disbursement or with-drawal of money from individuals, businesses, or taxpayers. Governments increase spending or decrease the money supply to stimulate growth during expansionary periods. Expansionary monetary policy, implemented by central banks, expands the money supply or lowers short-term interest rates. Central banks achieve this through open market operations, reserve requirements, and setting interest rates.

For instance, the U.S. Federal Reserve System, governed by the Board of Governors, proposes and reviews regulations to stimulate economic condi-tions. Government members, such as those in the House of Representatives or Senate, may vote on bills that alter tax policies. Once approved, these policies are communicated and implemented by relevant entities, such as the IRS for tax breaks or the Federal Reserve branches for monetary rates.

The Hazards of Expansionary Monetary Policy: Expansionary policy is a widely used tool to manage low-growth phases in the business cycle, but it carries inherent risks, including macroeconomic, microeconomic, and political economy concerns. Determining when to employ expansionary policy, its extent, and when to cease it necessitates sophisticated analysis involving significant uncertainties. Excessive expansion can lead to side effects such as high inflation or an overheated economy. The possible risks of expansionary policies are explained further below:

Risk of Outdated Analysis: An inherent challenge is the time lag between implementing a policy and its economic effects. Real-time analysis is nearly impossible due to this delay. Prudent decision-makers must discern when to halt or reverse expansionary measures to avoid high inflation, which might involve raising interest rates.

Risk of Macroeconomic Distortions: Expansionary fiscal and monetary poli-cies may create microeconomic distortions under ideal conditions. Economic models often oversimplify the impact, assuming the injected money spreads uniformly and instantly. However, these policies target specific individuals, businesses, and industries, leading to an effective transfer of purchasing power and wealth.

Risk of Corruption: Expansionary policies are susceptible to information and incentive problems inherent in government policies. Distributing funds into the economy may involve political considerations, potentially leading to issues like rent-seeking and principal-agent problems. Since expansionary policies deal with substantial public money, vigilance is essential to prevent corruption.

While deciding to expand or contract an economy lacks a clear signal, evaluating available data guides the action. This ambiguity often renders expansionary policy controversial, driven by subjective opinions.

Effects of Expansionary Policy: When a government enacts expansionary policy, its effects ripple through economies in various ways:

Interest Rates and Credit Availability: Lowering interest rates increases credit availability, fostering increased consumer spending and economic growth.

Business Activity and Investment: Expansionary policy stimulates business investment by reducing the cost of borrowing, leading to job creation and economic growth, resulting in more job openings.

Demand for Goods and Services: With increased consumer spending and business activity, there is a surge in demand for goods and services, often improving manufacturing information and leading to more balanced trade.

However, the primary negative consequence of expansionary policy is inflation. While aimed at reducing unemployment, the increase in the money supply can lead to inflation if it surpasses economic growth, causing higher prices, wages, and input costs.

Examples of Expansionary Policy

Major instances of expansionary policy include responses to the 2008 financial crisis, where central banks globally lowered interest rates and initiated stimulus spending. The U.S. implemented measures like the American Recovery and Reinvestment Act and multiple rounds of quantitative easing. In another example, Canada employed expansionary monetary policy by reducing interest rates during the economic slowdown caused by declining oil prices from 2014 to 2016. However, while boosting economic growth, this policy also negatively impacted bank profits. Also, amid the COVID-19 pandemic, governments worldwide embraced extreme expansionary policies. Lowering interest rates, issuing economic impact payments, and engaging in open market operations were prominent measures to counteract the economic halt.

Governments can pursue expansionary fiscal policy, increasing spending and lowering taxes to encourage consumer spending, or contractionary fiscal policy, involving spending cuts and tax increases to reduce aggregate demand. Examples from the U.K.'s past decade illustrate the impact of fiscal policy. In 2009, a cut in Value Added Tax (VAT) aimed to boost consumer spending, increasing government borrowing. In contrast, 2010 saw austerity measures with reduced government borrowing through spending cuts. Fiscal policy directly affects businesses by determining VAT and corporate tax bills. It also ripples the wider economy by influencing consumer spending on goods and services. Both monetary and fiscal policies affect small businesses and the broader economy. Tighter fiscal policy contracts the economy, reducing spending and demand and prompting business owners to plan accordingly.

Fiscal Policy in Response to the Coronavirus Crisis: Strengthening Confidence and Resilience

The COVID-19 outbreak necessitated decisive action to address health and economic crises. Governments globally have rapidly implemented economic policy responses, focusing on liquidity support for businesses and income support for vulnerable households. Multilateral collaboration and coordination are crucial to enhance the effectiveness of responses and bolster global economic resilience. Immediate measures have been aimed at preserving business cash flow, income, and employment. These include tax filing extensions, tax payment deferrals, loss offset provisions, and worker support through schemes like short-time work. As the crisis evolves, policy adaptation is essential, transitioning from support to stimulus for economic recovery. International coordination, financial support for developing countries, and flexibility in international standards are critical for an effective global response.

Policy Response During Containment and Mitigation

As containment and mitigation measures persist, the need for adapting policies to swiftly changing circumstances remains paramount. Tax policy should continue to focus on alleviating hardship while preserving the potential for a rapid economic rebound. This phase calls for precise adjustments and potential expansion of already implemented policies, recognizing that the costs of policy actions, though high, outweigh the greater costs of inaction.

Protecting Household Income and Employment: Safeguarding household income and employment remains crucial during the prolonged containment and mitigation phase. Extended measures may be necessary, with special attention to supporting the self-employed and those in the informal sector. Governments may consider providing extended wage and income support to mitigate the long-term impacts on households and businesses.

Addressing Business Risks: As the crisis persists, businesses face evolving risks, including solvency issues. Policies should adapt to these changing risks, potentially extending deferrals, implementing expanded loss carry-backs for loss-making firms, and expediting VAT refunds. It is essential to design these measures carefully to avoid increasing non-compliance risks.

Targeted Tax Support: Tax support should be precisely targeted to assist those in greatest need. While administratively demanding, targeted support can enhance outcomes by directing stronger assistance where it is most urgent. Priority sectors, especially small and medium-sized enterprises facing liquidity and solvency risks, should be considered. Focusing on businesses with pronounced employment risks can also help mitigate adverse impacts on households and aggregate demand.

Fiscal Stimulus for Recovery: To bolster recovery after containment and mitigation, sustained and adaptive support is essential. Debt payments may impede consumption and investment, and supply shocks may persist. A case for maintaining expansionary fiscal policy arises, stimulating broader household consumption and business investment. Efforts should be meticulously timed and well-targeted to prevent prolonged support in sectors where it is no longer needed.

International Policy Coordination: Policy coordination enhances the effectiveness of stimulus measures. Countries with the least impact and ample room for action can create positive feedback loops through trade and investment links, contributing to global economic recovery. This collaboration not only aids economic revival but also reduces the likelihood of virus flare-ups.

Exploring Tax Policy Post-Crisis: Given the anticipated reduction in tax revenues over several years, tax policy can restore public finances. Timely measures, alongside other policies, can smooth the financial costs of the crisis. The unique nature of the crisis prompts a reassessment of existing tax measures and the contemplation of new ones, such as solidarity levies and carbon taxes. The progressivity of the overall tax system is a key consideration.

Digitalization and Tax Challenges: Post-crisis, addressing the tax challenges posed by digitalization and ensuring a minimum level of tax payment by multinational enterprises will gain prominence. Ongoing work within the Inclusive Framework on BEPS focuses on these challenges, aligning with changing global economic circumstances.

International Support for Developing Countries: The crisis underscores the collective vulnerability of nations and the mutual benefits of enhancing global resilience. Developing countries, facing deeper human and economic impacts, require a new scale of support. International cooperation can aid in restructuring and canceling debts, rebuilding economies, and developing tax systems for universal healthcare. Efforts in property, carbon, progressive income taxes, and digital tax administration can significantly contribute to resource mobilization, with international cooperation providing financing and expertise.

Ongoing International Efforts: The international community's response to the COVID-19 crisis necessitates sustained support, debt restructuring, and reforms to ensure long-term resilience. Recognizing progress and identifying further measures to address challenges faced by low-income and low-capacity countries in international tax remains essential. The Inclusive Framework should continue its efforts, combining financing and expertise to support these countries comprehensively.

Corporate Taxation and Business Investment

In addressing weak investment in OECD countries post-global financial crisis, this analysis explores the link between corporate taxation and business investment. Despite a decline in the cost of capital, business investment rates have not risen, indicating other factors influencing investment decisions. While the cost of capital traditionally influences investment, other factors such as demand, financing, uncertainty, and market regulation play significant roles. Recent tax policy reforms in advanced economies suggest continued reliance on corporate tax measures. Understanding how firms react to tax reforms and which tax instruments effectively support growth is crucial for policymaking. Beyond statutory tax rates, measures affecting the tax base, such as capital allowances, could be more effective. The study disentangles various parameters of the corporate tax system to analyze the potential impacts of different tax designs. Understanding the heterogeneity in tax sensitivity contributes to effective policymaking.

Business investment plays a crucial role in determining productivity and long-term economic growth. Although corporate tax systems have traditionally been viewed as effective tools for supporting investment, a detailed empirical analysis is essential to understand how firms might respond to various tax reforms and which tax instruments are most effective in promoting investment.

In the aftermath of the Global Financial Crisis (GFC), business investment has been sluggish despite a decline in the cost of capital. Real gross investment has struggled to reach pre-GFC levels, with an overall lacklustre performance. Macro-level investment trends are primarily influenced by changes within sectors rather than shifts in the importance of low-investment-rate sectors.

The cost of capital has significantly decreased over the past two decades, mainly due to falling interest rates, but corporate taxation has also played a role in reducing it. Interestingly, investment is concentrated among a few large firms, often affiliated with multinational groups.

Investment patterns vary among firms, with large and young firms displaying more robust investment post-GFC than small and old firms. The tax sensitivity of investment has weakened since the GFC, but this effect differs across dimensions. Nonetheless, business investment generally responds negatively to increases in corporate taxation, as shown in past OECD analyses. However, the tax sensitivity of investment has decreased post-GFC. Differences in tax sensitivity are observed across asset types and firms, with large, multinational, highly profitable, and intangible-heavy firms being less sensitive to taxation. Effective tax rates (ETRs) influence investment differently based on tax instruments. Non-profit taxes have a more pronounced negative impact on business investment than corporate income tax (CIT). Changes in CIT statutory tax rates (STR) and capital allowances lead to varying investment responses, depending on the initial STR and allowances.

To support investment through CIT policies effectively, policymakers could consider options such as reducing non-profit taxes, limiting cuts in the headline STR, and using targeted CIT instruments for specific investments. However, targeted measures should carefully weigh the potential positive externalities against induced distortions and increased compliance costs, considering the impact of the Global Minimum Tax.

In summary, business investment has been subdued since the GFC despite a decline in the cost of capital. Various factors, including changes in investment rates within sectors and the heterogeneity among firms, contribute to this trend. Policymakers may enhance the effectiveness of CIT policies by accounting for the evolving tax sensitivity of different firms and considering targeted measures to support specific investments.

Sensitivity of Investment to Corporate Taxation: The sensitivity of investment to corporate taxation varies across firms, assets, and tax policy designs. Corporate income taxes typically hurt business investment, affecting after-tax returns and influencing firms to reconsider, scale down, or relocate certain investment projects. The sensitivity of firm investment to corporate tax rates differs based on various firm characteristics, such as size, age, sector, investment financing structure, liquidity constraints, market power, tax planning possibilities, and profitability.

Business investment exhibits sensitivity to corporate tax, but this sensitivity decreases over time. The tax sensitivity of investment has notably diminished post-GFC, as indicated by a positive and statistically significant coefficient of the time-dummy interacted variable. Industry-level investment also shows sensitivity to taxation on an extensive margin. The decline in tax sensitivity of investment over time could be influenced by factors not considered in the model, such as increased economic uncertainty, tightened access to finance, and rising market concentration. The tax sensitivity of investment varies over time depending on firm type. Large firms, those part of multinational groups, firms with a significant proportion of intangibles in their total fixed assets, and highly profitable firms have become less sensitive to taxation after 2009. The tax sensitivity of old firms has also weakened over time compared to young firms.

The characteristics of large, multinational, intangible-intensive, and profitable firms, often termed "superstar firms," contribute to their lower sensitivity to changes in corporate taxation. These firms, known for their productivity and innovation, may react differently due to market dominance, reluctance to reduce future investments threatening their position, and ample financial resources that make them less credit-constrained. Stimulating investment through statutory tax rate reductions may be less effective than previously assessed, and the paper highlights dimensions of heterogeneity in tax sensitivities that are crucial for CIT policy considerations.

Review Questions

1. How does fiscal policy differ from monetary policy, and what are the distinctive tools employed by each?
2. Explain the collaboration between the executive and legislative branches in the U.S. for implementing fiscal policy.
3. What are the main objectives of fiscal policy, and how do they vary based on economic circumstances?
4. Discuss the response strategies governments adopted during the 2007–2008 Great Recession, emphasizing the role of automatic stabilizers.
5. What are the risks associated with expansionary policies, and how can policymakers address these concerns?
6. How do governments balance the need for timely and targeted stimulus with concerns about deficits and debt sustainability?

Discussion Points

1. Collaboration in Economic Policy: Explore the advantages and challenges of having collaborative efforts between the executive and legislative branches in fiscal policy decision-making.
2. Long-Term Impacts of Fiscal Policy: Discuss the potential long-term effects of fiscal policy on income distribution, resource allocation, and overall economic well-being.
3. Global Cooperation in Economic Crises: Evaluate the importance of international collaboration and coordination in responding to global economic crises, using the COVID-19 pandemic as a case study.

CHAPTER THREE: TAX POLICY RESPONSES TO THE DUAL CHALLENGES OF HEALTH AND ECONOMIC CRISIS

Summary of Key Points

1. Unprecedented Challenges: The COVID-19 pandemic has led to a health crisis with profound economic repercussions. Policymakers have faced the challenge of balancing public health and economic stability amid uncertainties, including the emergence of new virus strains.

2. Four Policy Response: The policy response framework encompasses four phases - initial response, sustained efforts during containment, recovery, and restoring public finances. Each phase requires tailored tax policies, from preserving liquidity to restoring fiscal stability.

3. Assessment of Recent Measures: A review of measures across OECD, G20, and non-OECD non-G20 countries reveals a focus on emergency responses, predominantly tax deferrals, to support businesses and households. Fiscal package size and variations across countries affect public budgets and debt levels.

4. Strategies to Support Businesses: The emphasis on prioritizing business cash flow involves a mix of tax and non-tax measures. Tax tools such as deferring tax payments and introducing targeted waivers aim to enhance liquidity. The degree of policy targeting varies across countries and sectors.

5. Household Support Measures: Countries implement diverse measures to boost household cash flow, including tax filing extensions, deferrals, and direct cash transfers. Support is tailored to target vulnerable groups, and the design of measures varies widely among nations.

6. Investment and Consumption Support: Some countries introduce measures to support investment and consumption, such as tax incentives and VAT rate reductions. These measures are more prevalent in countries facing less severe impacts and during the early stages of the crisis.

The Policy Landscape in the Face of Unprecedented Challenges: Simultaneous Health and Economic Crisis

The COVID-19 has triggered a health crisis with unparalleled economic repercussions. Authorities have rightfully prioritized the containment of the virus to mitigate the impact on public health. Widespread containment and mitigation measures have been implemented across nations, significantly affecting economic activity. The OECD estimates suggest a substantial initial decline in economic activity, emphasizing the unpredictability of these impacts. The uncertainty surrounding the pandemic's trajectory adds complexity. Even after vaccines have been developed, the human and economic toll has only eased a little as newer virus stains keep emerging. The evolving dynamics have warranted a reinstatement of containment measures in some areas, posing challenging trade-offs. Since 2020, economists and policymakers have been under immense pressure to articulate clear objectives and maintain public confidence amid uncertainties to tackle the pandemic's changing faces.

Policy Objectives Amid the Pandemic: The immediate challenge was to bolster the health crisis response by enhancing healthcare systems and accelerating the development of tests, treatments, and vaccines. Simultaneously, steps were taken to mitigate the adverse effects of containment measures on households and businesses. In particular, efforts were made to maintain economic stability while shielding the vulnerable. It was also necessary to facilitate a swift economic recovery with marching stimulus programs.

Enhancing the resilience of economic and health systems was paramount for nearly all countries by incorporating mechanisms for early epidemic response, economic shock absorption, and supply chain resilience.

Evolution of Policy Responses

The policy response framework can be delineated into four overarching phases: the initial outbreak response, sustained efforts during containment and mitigation, recovery, and the eventual restoration of public finances. Each phase necessitates tailored tax policies, outlined in subsequent sections.

Phase 1: Initial Response – Preserving Liquidity and Income Support: Countries employ tax systems to swiftly provide financial support to businesses and households in this phase. These comprised coordinated fiscal, monetary, health, and financial measures. Emphasis is on maintaining business liquidity and supporting household income through short-term measures such as tax deferrals, waivers, and financial support. The focus is minimizing immediate hardship caused by containment measures and facilitating a rapid economic rebound.

Phase 2: Sustained Efforts During Containment and Mitigation – Adapting to New Realities: Tax policies need broader and more sustained responses as containment and mitigation persist. The focus shifts to fine-tuning and potentially expanding existing policies to address evolving risks. Businesses face liquidity-to-solvency risks, requiring adaptive measures such as extended tax payment deferrals, social security contribution waivers, and wage payment support.

Phase 3: Recovery – Stimulus for Investment and Consumption: With economic recovery in sight, fiscal stimulus became crucial to reignite investment and consumption. Corporations and households may grapple with increased debt, closures, and uncertainty, necessitating strategic tax policies to stimulate consumption and investment. The transition from Phase 2 to Phase 3 was largely non-linear, requiring careful removal of short-term measures.

Phase 4: Restoring Public Finances – Balancing Growth and Sustainability:

As economies stabilize, attention shifts to restoring public finances. Governments face financial strain from support measures, prompting considerations for revenue-raising initiatives. The timing and execution of revenue-raising measures are critical to align with long-term growth, inclusivity, and sustainability objectives.

This framework has guided countries in tailoring tax policies across diverse pandemic phases, recognizing the nuanced challenges and evolving dynamics.

Assessment of Recent Measures in Response to COVID-19

This evaluation includes OECD and G20 countries, non-OECD, non-G20 emerging markets, and developing economies. The data is drawn from an OECD database compiling tax and broader fiscal policy responses to the crisis.

Overview of Short-Term Measures: Countries have predominantly focused on emergency responses to address the acute impact of the crisis on businesses and households while sustaining economic capacity. The primary objectives of fiscal packages include:

1. Globally align mitigating the impact of containment measures,
2. Ensuring the quick resumption of economic activities during a health crisis and
3. Providing essential support to businesses and households.

Businesses receive liquidity support to maintain their viability, while individuals, particularly the most affected households, receive income support. Concurrently, measures have been implemented to enhance the healthcare sector's functionality and funding. These rapid responses were often predicated on the assumption of shorter containment phases than what has unfolded. Most measures are immediate and time-limited. Although commonly labeled as "fiscal stimulus," these actions are better characterized as emergencies or initial responses. Traditional fiscal stimulus promoting investment and consumption may be more effective under a crisis, especially when there are seriously enforced restriction mandates, as strong commitments to production initiatives may risk virus spread.

Business Support Measures: Similarities exist across countries in the measures supporting businesses, primarily emphasizing tax payment deferrals. The adoption or expansion of short-time work schemes is also widespread. Noteworthy differences emerge in measures supporting households, with the United States opting for direct cash transfers. At the same time, European countries simplify access to paid sick leave and unemployment benefits, particularly for non-standard workers. Developing and emerging countries, less directly affected and constrained in fiscal space, have been less active. Social assistance measures, including cash transfers, are more prevalent than social insurance or short-time work schemes, with several developing countries introducing tax payment deferrals.

Fiscal Package Size and Variations: Fiscal packages exhibit substantial variations in size, with some countries, such as Germany, the United Kingdom, and the United States, taking unprecedented actions. The budgetary effects differ widely, encompassing permanent losses (e.g., short-time work schemes) and temporary impacts on budget balances (deferrals, filing extensions, loss offsets). Though not incurring a direct fiscal cost, state loans and loan guarantees generate contingent liabilities with potential future expenses. These cost estimates focus on the immediate revenue impact of relief measures, excluding longer-term tax revenue consequences and the costs associated with future fiscal stimulus measures. The persistence of the economic situation may lead to extending certain measures and altering cost dynamics. Current estimates may need to capture the impending tax policy challenges fully, contingent on GDP and key aggregate evolution. The fiscal packages will likely affect public budgets and debt levels across countries.

Strategies to Support Businesses

Prioritizing Business Cash Flow: Countries have predominantly directed their efforts towards fortifying business cash flow, recognizing numerous enterprises' acute decline in liquidity. This liquidity challenge hampers their ability to meet critical expenses like wages, rents, intermediate goods, interest on debt, and taxes. Measures have been strategically designed to address these cash flow issues, aiming to avert undesirable outcomes such as layoffs, temporary financial incapacity, and, in extreme cases, business closures or bankruptcies. The interconnected nature of businesses means that cash flow challenges can trigger a domino effect, leading to the failure of multiple businesses. Approximately half of the globally reported measures have focused on enhancing business cash flow.

Diverse Support Measures for Cash Flow: Tax and non-tax measures have been deployed to provide comprehensive support for cash flow challenges. Non-tax measures are primarily characterized by loan guarantee schemes, where governments pledge to guarantee part or all of the value of bank loans granted to eligible businesses. Small interest-free loans and cash grants, particularly targeted at small businesses or those in severely affected sectors, are also prevalent non-tax tools. Some countries, such as the Slovak Republic, Sweden, and the United States, have implemented deferrals for non-wage business costs like rent or interest.

Tax Measures to Enhance Business Cash Flow: Within the realm of tax measures, the most widely used tool for improving business cash flow has been the deferral of tax payments. Seventy-five percent of OECD and G20 countries have implemented such deferrals, primarily focused on taxes requiring frequent payments. These include advance corporate income tax (CIT) or personal income tax (PIT) payments, value-added tax (VAT), and social security contributions (SSCs). Additionally, 28 percent of these countries extended filing deadlines for business taxpayers. Notable tax policy tools include modifications to loss-offset provisions, allowing loss carry-back, or extending loss-carry forward periods in certain countries.

Targeted Tax Waivers and Administrative Measures: Some countries enacted measures to ease the tax burden on businesses during the health crisis. These measures concentrated mainly on tax categories unaffected by immediate economic cycles, reducing potential hardship for businesses facing significant revenue losses. Common waivers encompass social security contributions, property taxes, and presumptive taxes for small businesses.

Specific levies on tourism and airline companies and reduced import taxes on select sectors have been introduced in some instances. Widespread tax administration measures include accelerated tax refunds and more flexible tax debt repayment plans.

Diverse Policy Targeting: The degree of policy targeting exhibits variation across countries, sectors, and businesses. Measures are occasionally universally accessible, sector-specific, or tailored for businesses experiencing a substantial revenue drop. Some countries adopt a case-by-case approach, necessitating businesses to seek support explicitly. A discernible trend in certain countries involves targeting small and medium-sized enterprises (SMEs) or self-employed businesses, anticipating higher liquidity constraints. Tax payment deferrals are the most common measure in non-OECD, non-G20 developing and emerging economies, accounting for 45 percent of total measures. Filing extensions and more flexible tax debt repayment plans were also widely adopted. A few countries, especially in the tourism sector, introduced tax waivers.

Measures for Job Retention: Numerous OECD and G20 countries implemented, extended, or expanded eligibility for short-time work schemes to mitigate substantial job losses. These schemes provide public income support to workers facing reduced working hours or temporary layoffs, with firms maintaining employee contracts. The intention is to retain talent and experience, enabling a swift recovery in production once economic conditions improve. The generosity and coverage of these schemes exhibit significant variability among countries, with many European nations offering particularly generous schemes. Some countries also extend unemployment benefits to those temporarily unemployed or working reduced hours, provided they remain employed. The application of these measures varied across countries, with some implementing broad measures and others adopting a more targeted approach, focusing on small employers or severely affected sectors. Short-time work schemes and wage subsidies for employers are less common outside of the OECD and G20, with exceptions like Peru and Thailand, where Peru introduced a wage subsidy equal to 35 percent of the payroll for qualifying employers with workers earning less than approximately USD 430.

Household Support Measures

Various countries have implemented measures to boost households' cash flow. These include extending tax filing deadlines, deferring tax payments, or providing extended payment plans for households facing difficulties meeting their tax obligations. These measures predominantly apply to personal income taxes, with some countries also addressing property taxes. Certain nations, like Chile, targeted low-income households or properties below a specified value with tax payment deferral measures. Other tax measures include expediting refunds for excess personal income tax payments and offering flexible arrangements for tax debt repayments, often geared towards lower-income individuals. Non-tax measures encompass early superannuation release in Australia, deferral interest payments on mortgage debt for primary residences in Spain, and deferral utility bill payments.

Income Support through Cash Benefits: Most countries focus on increasing cash benefits to provide income support for vulnerable households. Many OECD and G20 nations already have social protection systems that offer income replacement for households affected by sickness, job loss, or earnings reduction. Given the severity of the crisis, the existing efforts were expanded to cover previously excluded groups or cases. The support primarily involves direct transfers rather than utilizing the tax system. The need for rapid drives this choice and targeted financial assistance to the most vulnerable households during the crisis.

Diverse Targeting and Design: These measures' targeted households and designs vary among countries. Cash transfers may specifically target those directly affected by the virus or its immediate economic consequences, such as sick or temporarily unemployed workers. Some measures extend support to the self-employed, as seen in Italy, Lithuania, and the United Kingdom. Other countries provide cash payments to low-income households more broadly. Chile, for instance, introduced a cash bonus benefiting people who need formal work. Some benefits are aimed at families, including increases in child benefits. These benefits can be one-off payments or temporary increases in regular benefits, like New Zealand's temporary change to its in-work tax credit.

Support in Developing Countries: In non-OECD, non-G20 emerging markets, and developing countries, some have reported cash transfers targeting vulnerable households, as seen in Kenya, or distributing more broadly to low-income households, as in Peru. Additional measures include a 30 percent reduction in personal income tax rates for individual entrepreneurs in Uzbekistan engaged in the tourism sector.

Expanding Sick Leave and Unemployment Benefits: About 30 percent of OECD and G20 countries have expanded sick leave benefits, with some countries easing access conditions and expanding eligibility, including covering a larger portion of benefits, reducing the burden on employers. Some countries, like New York State, impose new requirements in the absence of generally applicable obligations for employers to provide sick leave. Over a third of OECD and G20 countries have expanded unemployment benefit coverage, often extending benefits to self-employed workers and those in non-standard employment. Some countries also expanded unemployment benefits to workers in quarantine.

Global Variations in Job Retention Measures in Developing Countries: Emerging markets and developing countries outside the OECD and the G20 have not reported any sick leave or unemployment benefits expansions, which may be attributed to less developed social protection systems, primarily relying on cash transfers to support households.

Investment and Consumption Support Measures

A few OECD and G20 countries introduced measures to support investment and consumption. Investment support measures include temporary threshold increases for low-value asset write-offs and accelerated depreciation in countries like Australia and New Zealand. Indonesia has temporarily waived or exempted import taxes for manufacturing companies in 19 sectors. Italy introduced a corporate tax credit for sanitation costs in workplaces. Some countries, including China, Cyprus, and Norway, attempted to support consumption through temporary reductions in standard and reduced VAT rates.

Support measures for investment and consumption were more prevalent in countries outside the OECD and G20. For example, Kenya reduced its corporate and top personal income tax rates. Jamaica and Kenya lowered their standard VAT rates to support consumption. Some countries also decreased their reduced VAT rates, as seen in Moldova and Kazakhstan. Generally, investment and consumption support measures were typically implemented in countries facing less severe impacts or during the early stages of the crisis, preceding stringent containment measures. Their immediate effectiveness might be diminished in nations where lockdowns coincided with these measures.

Measures to Bolster the Healthcare Sector's Response to COVID-19

Apart from containment and mitigation efforts, countries adopted measures to reinforce patient care and alleviate pressure on healthcare systems. Several OECD and G20 nations facilitated the import of medical inputs to combat COVID-19. Common measures included temporarily lifting import duties on medicines, health devices, and equipment, often accompanied by streamlined customs clearance. Some countries offered preferential tax treatment to boost health-related spending and investment, such as safeguarding input VAT deductions on donated items and enhancing the deductibility of donations for corporate and personal income tax purposes. China introduced specific corporate income tax incentives for enterprises producing key supplies related to COVID-19.

In non-OECD, non-G20 developing countries, measures supporting the healthcare sector were prevalent, mainly involving removing or reducing import duties and taxes on medical equipment. Additional initiatives included special allowances to medical personnel, lump-sum payments to health-care workers testing positive for COVID-19, and immigration staff benefits (Malaysia).

Challenges and the Role of Tax Policy During Containment

Extended containment measures exacerbate negative impacts on businesses and households, making it challenging for economic activity to rebound. Prolonged phases may lead to increased job losses, firm bankruptcies, and defaults on mortgages and loans. Developing countries face heightened challenges due to the withdrawal of investment, high population density, large informal sectors, weaker health and social protection systems, higher public debt, and currency depreciations. The immediate and substantial action mitigated long-term costs. Support measures for businesses and households were crucial for immediate relief and ensuring a swift economic rebound. Fiscal actions, coordinated with other policy levers, must learn from past crises and avoid premature contraction. Coordination between fiscal and monetary policy is essential, and central banks may play a role in supporting fiscal expansion. Also, developing countries, facing constraints in monetary policy and high debt risks, required international coordination for additional financing. Currency depreciations exacerbate debt financing challenges, necessitating international support to reduce the debt burden.

Lessons Learned from Adopted Measures

Observations from adopted measures indicate the importance of strong and timely actions targeting immediate relief and long-term economic resilience. Early interventions, coordination across policies, and adapting measures to evolving circumstances contribute to effectiveness. Governments must continuously monitor and adjust policies as containment measures persist. Suggested measures include:

1. Expanding expensing or depreciation allowances to support health-related objectives,
2. Ensuring coordination with other policy areas and
3. Managing corporate debt and access to credit.

Also, addressing challenges related to administration and implementation is vital for the successful execution of policies during containment. Governments must remain adaptable and responsive to evolving circumstances, ensuring effective and equitable policy implementation.

Key Insights from Countries' Tax Policy Responses: Many countries have swiftly implemented fiscal, monetary, and financial policies, adopting a phased strategy. The timing of tax policy responses was generally rapid, with some nations progressively extending relief packages as the crisis evolves, a prudent approach given the ongoing uncertainty. However, most measures were short-term or temporary, aligning with the phased approach and allowing regular reassessment. Explicitly signaling the temporary nature helps avoid pressure groups lobbying for permanent changes, maintaining flexibility. Time-bound deferrals of filing and reporting obligations ensure governments gather necessary data for ongoing crisis impact assessment.

Broad Approach and Benchmarking: International organizations like the UNDP and WHO have helped to midwife broad approaches and benchmarking frameworks to help countries employ a broad approach, utilizing a mix of fiscal and financial tools. Benchmarking support measures against other nations are advised to ensure comprehensive utilization of available policy levers, optimizing effectiveness. Generally, short-term measures supporting businesses, like liquidity support through tax deferrals, are considered appropriate. Tax deferrals offer timely cash flow support, especially for taxes payable within tight deadlines. Efforts to retain workers, proven effective during the 2008-09 recession, and rapid income support to affected households have been aptly incorporated.

Targeted Approach and Careful Design: Countries have mostly targeted measures to the most affected households and sectors, although targeting levels and types have varied. While targeted support reduces fiscal costs and avoids aiding unnecessary recipients, policymakers must ensure effectiveness through careful design. Announced measures, especially investment tax incentives and CIT rate reductions, must be effective and well-targeted to avoid unintended consequences. Countries are urged to automate support measures, particularly for SMEs, to streamline application processes. Considering potential abuse risks, exploring additional cash flow-oriented measures like accelerated VAT refunds and flexible VAT bad debt relief is advisable.

As the health crisis persists, existing measures can be fine-tuned or extended, and new ones may be considered. Liquidity risks evolving into solvency risks for businesses necessitate bolstering existing responses or introducing new ones. A greater focus on solvency risks, in addition to liquidity issues, is crucial. Governments can use the corporate tax system to support liquidity and solvency through deferrals and reductions in corporate tax liability. Targeted measures focusing on sectors severely affected by containment measures and providing greater support for SMEs may be instrumental. Unlimited tax deferrals, equivalent to interest-free loans, can be economically effective in supporting businesses. Leveraging the tax system for such support, with tax administrations possessing relevant information, can target a broader spectrum of firms more efficiently.

Consideration should be given to expanding loss-carry-back measures with extended time limits or increased refund ceilings, which can be impactful in targeting lossmaking firms that may not benefit from other tax measures, supporting SMEs, and countering the effects of the crisis. Equally, temporarily adjusting inventory valuation methods can incentivize multinational enterprises (MNEs) to build up stocks of crucial intermediate inputs to enhance the resilience of global value chains (GVCs) to future disruptions, making MNEs more robust. Temporary tax rate reductions or exemptions for specific businesses may be relevant for tax bases slow to shift downward. Targeting interventions to certain businesses, considering budgetary impacts, ensures efficient implementation. In summary, continuous and well-calibrated efforts are essential for evolving policy responses to address the dynamic challenges posed by the health crisis.

Review Questions

1. How does the pandemic's evolving nature impact policymakers' challenges in crafting effective tax policies?
2. What are the key differences in household support measures between

OECD, G20, and non-OECD, non-G20 countries?

3. Examine the variations in business support strategies and their effectiveness during different pandemic phases.

4. How do fiscal package variations across countries contribute to the overall global economic landscape, and what are the potential long-term consequences?

5. Evaluate the role of international organizations in guiding countries to employ effective tax policy responses and benchmarking against global standards.

6. Discuss the potential risks and benefits of temporary tax rate reductions and exemptions for specific businesses during a health and economic crisis.

Discussion Points

1. Global Coordination: To what extent is international coordination necessary for developing countries facing challenges in monetary policy and high debt risks?

2. Long-Term Resilience: How can tax policies be designed to enhance the long-term resilience of global value chains and businesses in the face of future disruptions?

3. Balancing Act: Discuss the challenges policymakers face in balancing implementing short-term emergency responses and planning for long-term fiscal sustainability.

CHAPTER FOUR: TAX POLICIES AND RESILIENCE-BUILDING FOR SPEEDY RECOVERY FROM THE COVID-19 PANDEMIC

Summary of Key Points

1. Liquidity Management: Explore strategies like deferring VAT payments, accelerating VAT refunds, and targeted subsidies to alleviate liquidity pressures for businesses during economic crises.

2. Social Protection Systems: Examine the role of short-time work schemes, unemployment benefits, and minimum-income support in stabilizing households and contributing to economic recovery.

3. Tax Administration Efficiency: Highlight the importance of swift support delivery, utilizing established channels, and considering alternative methods, especially in countries with large informal sectors.

4. Stimulus Measures: Discuss the design principles for effective stimulus packages, emphasizing inclusivity, temporary nature, and international coordination to enhance economic recovery.

5. Revenue Impacts and Fiscal Space: Analyze the anticipated global impact of COVID-19 on tax revenues, budget balances, and public debts, recognizing variations across countries and the need for innovative financing approaches.

6. Domestic Resource Mobilization: Emphasize the role of taxation, including property and carbon taxes, in long-term financing for public services, investment, and economic reconstruction, focusing on building effective tax systems in developing countries.

Alleviating Liquidity Pressures

To alleviate liquidity pressure and minimize subsequent solvency risks, subsidies and indirect tax measures, especially concerning VAT, are crucial. VAT payments are often due before businesses receive customer payments, intensifying cash flow challenges. Deferring VAT payments, temporary flexibility in VAT bad debt relief, and improved access to cash-accounting regimes can help mitigate these adverse impacts. Even when businesses receive VAT payments, deferring tax payments relieves cash flow pressure. Governments should also consider targeted measures, such as writing off or deferring payment of excise duties for vulnerable sectors like hospitality, ensuring precise targeting to prevent unnecessary revenue losses. Accelerating VAT refunds can enhance business cash flow, but carefully considering fraud risks is essential. While output VAT for many businesses decreases due to declining sales, input VAT on fixed costs continues to accrue, leading to excess input VAT credits. Governments can expedite the processing of VAT refund claims, enhancing administrative capacity while implementing risk-based compliance management to minimize refund fraud risks.

Tax measures supporting businesses should align with a country's economic development. Countries can adapt income taxes, social security contributions, VAT reductions, exemptions, subsidies, and deferrals based on their tax mix. However, if legal or practical constraints limit policy changes, adjustments in other taxes, like payroll or excise taxes, may be considered. Policymakers must carefully target these policies for optimal economic support and fiscal sustainability, especially in developing countries reliant on CIT or VAT from foreign MNEs, where support should be directed towards the domestic sector and SMEs for fiscal efficiency.

Additional Support Measures for Households: The ongoing crisis poses significant risks to households, with historic increases in unemployment observed in many countries. The unemployment decline is expected to be slower than its increase, requiring expanded wage and government income support. Maintaining workers in current jobs through short-time work schemes supports household spending, adherence to containment measures, and limits economic hardship. Social protection systems are crucial in stabilizing the economy by softening household income losses. Unemployment benefits and minimum-income benefits (social assistance) contribute to this stabilization. Public employment services should actively support jobless benefit recipients in job searches and skill development, anticipating a prolonged need for high public expenditures on social benefits. Short-term work schemes and wage support policies should consider non-standard workers and those in the informal sector. Extending support to these workers, who may not file tax returns regularly, helps maintain compliance with containment measures.

Countries with taxes on mobile money and money transfers could consider temporary waivers to encourage using mobile money over cash transactions, reducing infection risks. Reducing the costs of remittances, a vital financing source in many developing countries, could have a substantial impact, especially in Africa, where transaction costs are high. Coordinated action is essential to achieve these reductions and contribute to economic stability.

Considerations for Tax Administration and Implementation

Given the urgency and scale of the economic shock impacting businesses and households, swift support delivery is paramount. Utilizing established and proven channels for support distribution is advisable, emphasizing speed where multiple options exist. For instance, delivering income support to households through cash benefits might be quicker than using the tax system. Alternatively, a proposed approach is to provide broad income support without specific targeting, subjecting payments to regular taxation, ensuring low-income households receive the full support. In contrast, wealthier households contribute back through the tax system. Developing countries face unique challenges in delivering rapid and effective support, especially through the tax system. The prevalence of large informal sectors makes it challenging to implement measures like waving or deferring tax payments. In such cases, providing support directly to individuals and households through cash transfers, recurring minimum income, or energy and housing subsidies becomes crucial. Involving local authorities and leveraging simple online platforms can enhance visibility and accessibility.

Mitigating Unintended Adverse Effects: Efforts should be made to mitigate unintended adverse effects stemming from support measures. For example, decisions to defer tax reporting may impact refunds, leading to increased cash flow problems for taxpayers. Offering optional deferral of reporting obligations, coupled with prioritizing returns involving refund claims, can address these risks.

Limiting Non-Compliance Risks: Understandably, tax compliance tends to decline during a crisis driven by economic stress. Measures must be taken to limit non-compliance risks to prevent long-term declines in tax revenues. If not carefully managed, the deferral of tax payments and collections may be prone to abuse and fraud. Tax authorities should adhere to well-established risk-based compliance management principles tailored to the evolving circumstances of the pandemic. Targeted assistance, enforcement measures, and differentiated treatment based on compliance history are strategies to curb potential non-compliance.

Tailoring Crisis Response Measures: Crisis response measures should align with a country's administrative capacity and specific compliance risks. Developing economies, often grappling with limited revenue administration capacity and high informality, should tailor tax measures accordingly, which may involve limiting certain measures, like accelerated VAT refunds, to businesses with a good compliance history. Temporary measures can focus on crisis-specific issues, monitoring compliance indicators, and providing targeted assistance to selected taxpayers. Proactive outreach and effective communication with taxpayers can contribute to long-term compliance improvements.

Tax Policy During the Recovery Stage of the Crisis

As the world was recovering from the initial hit of the COVID-19 pandemic, the tax policy options for best-practice countries focused on judiciously phasing out some short-term measures and directing stimulus efforts where they can be most impactful. In scenarios where recovery is sluggish, a more extended period of expansionary fiscal policy was deployed to stimulate aggregate demand further. The health crisis led to an economic downturn beyond sectors directly affected by containment and mitigation measures. Debt accumulated during containment may reduce consumption unless repayment is shifted forward. An expansionary fiscal approach could prioritize reducing taxes that impede clean and inclusive growth while avoiding windfall gains to businesses and households.

The transition from containment to recovery is anticipated to be gradual and varied across countries. The relaxation of containment measures might differ by activity type, location, or age group. While economic activities may gradually resume, certain sectors, such as tourism and hospitality, could face ongoing severe restrictions. The transition might also be intermittent, involving cycles of relaxation and tightening based on fluctuating outbreak risks. This variability poses potential risks of uneven effects on businesses and households, necessitating careful consideration in national policy responses. As economies recuperate, reassessing short-term measures becomes crucial for revitalizing economic dynamism. Extended support for households, particularly through unemployment benefits, may unintentionally impede labor market activation. Similarly, prolonged wage support might discourage necessary staff turnover, particularly in countries with traditionally high net replacement rates of unemployment benefits. Continued support for businesses might sustain 'zombie' firms that would only survive with containment measures, and tax reductions and deferrals could harm medium-term revenue-raising capacity.

Short-term measures must be removed carefully to prevent sudden spikes in tax liabilities. Measures like tax deferrals, when removed, should be structured to avoid creating cliff edges that could lead to solvency problems for recovering businesses and undermine the overall recovery, involving spreading tax payments over several tax years, averaging tax bases for turnover taxes or social security contributions, and incorporating carry-forward provisions for corporate taxes.

Coexistence of Containment and Recovery Policies: The coexistence of containment and recovery policies is a reality. The exit from the crisis may be complex, with containment and mitigation measures persisting, reinstated, or partially de-confined. The pace and extent of relaxation differ across countries and regions, leading to enduring supply shocks and reduced business productivity. Therefore, the mix of containment and recovery-oriented support measures should align closely with the nature of the containment and mitigation measures. For example, businesses subject to ongoing containment and mitigation measures, even with partial relaxation for other sectors, may require sustained liquidity and solvency support. If containment measures are lifted unexpectedly swiftly, the economy may have substantial pent-up demand. Policymakers must monitor and adjust stimulus measures to prevent excessive inflation from a combination of pent-up demand and stimulus measures, especially relevant in countries with weaker governance, historically higher inflation, and more volatile currency values.

Implementing effective stimulus measures for recovery hinges on bolstering demand for consumption and investment goods. Policymakers need to establish conditions that fortify both consumption and investment. Tailoring stimulus packages to individual countries becomes imperative based on the output gap resulting from the crisis. Fiscal stimulus packages should be temporary and well-communicated to avoid creating permanent deficits. Effective communication ensures that the stimulus encourages demand rather than merely servicing existing debt or boosting savings. For more inclusivity, household support should be directed towards less affluent households. Research indicates that lower-income households are more likely to spend additional disposable income received through fiscal stimulus packages, providing a higher multiplier effect than the more affluent households. Attention should be given to reaching groups not well-covered by standard fiscal tools, particularly those primarily active in the informal economy.

Stimulus measures should support a swift recovery while avoiding windfall gains. Consideration could be given to measures like accelerated depreciation allowances. At the same time, tax cuts for capital income and gains and broad corporate income tax (CIT) reductions may be less effective. Policy-makers should steer clear of provisions causing only timing differences in consumption or investment with limited impact on aggregate behavior, such as reductions in capital gains taxes.

Coordination across countries enhances the effectiveness of stimulus efforts. While the costs of the crisis will not be uniform across nations, collective action is essential. Uncoordinated or unilateral action could exacerbate overall social and economic costs. International collaboration, with countries contributing in line with their relative economic strength, can be more effective in containing the economic crisis. Early, large, or isolated stimulus actions may lead to funding difficulties or currency mismatches, highlighting the importance of international institutions in coordinating stimulus policies (OECD, 2020[32]).

Ensuring an Inclusive Recovery: The unequal exposure to health and financial risks demands policy attention to prevent worsening inequalities. Policies can contribute by providing continued and targeted support to low-income households, leveraging proven mechanisms like earned income tax credits and tax credits for low-income families with children. This targeted support not only aids economic recovery but also aligns with the likelihood that lower-income households will spend additional income. It must be stressed that inclusive recovery is hastened when more efforts are directed at supporting those often overlooked by standard systems, including informal workers and people experiencing homelessness. Policies can reduce the vulnerability of self-employed and gig workers, who typically lack the same level of social protection as regular employees. The crisis has spotlighted their vulnerability, and temporary expansions of sick leave or unemployment benefits may need to be considered for these workers, potentially leading to longer-term improvements in their social protection.

Moreover, policies must address the damage inflicted on labor markets. Reducing unemployment is not just a consequence but an enabler of economic recovery. Expanded active labor market policies may be warranted, particularly in sectors where unemployment has risen significantly.

Pooling Resources to Support Developing Countries: International cooperation becomes crucial to support developing countries. The pandemic has underscored the interconnectedness of all countries, emphasizing the need for global resilience. Developing nations require special support to enhance their resilience against future pandemics, necessitating international collaboration. While progress has been made in international tax cooperation, especially in developed countries, further efforts are needed, including financial support and assistance in building digitalized tax systems, to ensure effective taxation of cross-border activities and offshore assets in low-income and low-capacity countries, involving a review of international standards and instruments.

As economic support measures implemented during containment and mitigation are phased out, there is a need to stimulate investment more. Accelerated depreciation allowances or similar investment incentives can support domestic investment, specifically in the health and economic crisis severely impacted sectors. Tailoring differentiated recovery measures might be necessary, acknowledging potential catch-up growth in manufacturing sectors, whereas the services sector, particularly tourism, may experience a slower recovery. Specific support for individual entrepreneurs and small business owners in developing countries' origin is crucial, involving facilitating a fair division of economic losses in bankruptcy cases or supporting the establishment of new businesses. Such measures should align closely with credit and financial policies. Awarding favorable tax treatment for investments with positive social spill-over effects, especially in research and development and resilience-building, could be considered. Governance plays a pivotal role in designing incentives for resilience, with developing countries needing to focus on effective tax incentives while avoiding unnecessary measures. Increased transparency and international coordination can mitigate the risks of imprudent incentives.

Strengthening Resilience

Recovery-phase policies can contribute to building resilience against future health crises. Strengthening disease surveillance, adaptable health systems, and the development of diagnostics, treatments, and vaccines are essential. Universal health coverage emerges as a key element for health system resilience, necessitating additional public investment in the healthcare sector. Combining tools, such as automatic stabilizers and investment incentives, can enhance resilience to economic shocks. Measures providing greater social protection to non-standard workers can reduce their exposure to future risks. Recovery policies also offer opportunities to align with environmental objectives, using tax incentives to support environmental commitments in pollution-intensive sectors.

Revenue Impacts of Containment and Mitigation: The direct impact of COVID-19 on tax revenues, even before considering fiscal policy responses, is poised to be significant globally. Economic slowdowns and employment reductions will lead to lower income tax collections, corporate income tax, and reduced consumption tax revenues. Reduced tourism, falling resource prices (especially oil), and changes in consumer behavior will further impact revenues. Estimating the impact on global GDP remains speculative, but early indicators suggest a substantial impact on tax revenues. Revenue impacts will vary across countries and depend on their tax mix. Developing countries may face more pronounced revenue impacts due to heavy reliance on trade taxes, commodity revenues, and vulnerability to fluctuations in global demand.

Impact on Budget Balances and Public Debts: The crisis is expected to impact budget balances and public debt levels substantially. The combined effects of fiscal packages, increased public spending, and reduced tax revenues will lead to significant government borrowing, resulting in deteriorating budget balances and higher public debt levels. Budget deficits and high debt levels could have severe consequences, but certain countries have some fiscal space. Net government interest payments as a share of GDP are generally below post-GFC levels, indicating room for maneuver in several countries. Countries' fiscal positions heading into the crisis varied, and fiscal space is generally smaller in developing countries. Innovative approaches to financing and funding are needed, with international institutions and development aid playing a critical role in ensuring access to finance at sustainable rates, especially for low-income countries facing challenging fiscal positions.

Exploring Tax Policy Reform

Tax policy plays a crucial role in covering the costs of the crisis and related policy responses. As countries consider restoring public finances, the timing of such efforts is important, recognizing that some countries may face a prolonged path to recovery. The role of tax extends beyond revenue levels, encompassing the structure that might require adaptation in a post-COVID era. Policymakers should prioritize supporting robust growth through sustained stimulus measures, recognizing that solid growth contributes to expanding tax revenues, which can be complemented by policies to manage costs over time, such as central banks retaining government bonds on their balance sheets. The crisis's unprecedented nature prompts reflection on whether exceptional measures, akin to post-wars or major fiscal crises, could be considered. Proposals include exploring new revenue sources or modifying existing tax systems.

Some scholars and stakeholders suggest extraordinary revenue-raising measures, such as taxing additional income earned during the crisis or implementing carbon pricing tax measures for long-term structural reform. Though acknowledging political challenges, there is evidence that introducing new taxes during major policy reforms may be more feasible. International cooperation could further facilitate the introduction or strengthening of carbon pricing. Reforms of the current tax landscape, like base broadening measures and addressing inefficient tax expenditures, could be reconsidered within a broader tax system review. Governments might also explore new or under-used tax bases, focusing on those least detrimental to growth, such as recurrent taxes on immovable property and general consumption taxes. Analytical work is necessary, recognizing that efforts to restore public finances are yet to begin.

Corporate Income Taxation and the International Tax Agenda: Since the 2008 global crisis, international tax cooperation has progressed significantly, addressing tax transparency and fighting tax avoidance by multinational enterprises (MNEs). Efforts under the Inclusive Framework on BEPS focus on two pillars: reallocating taxing rights (Pillar 1) and ensuring MNE profits are subject to a minimum level of tax (Pillar 2). Despite disruptions due to the health crisis, progress continues, and post-crisis, addressing digitalization challenges and ensuring MNEs pay a minimum tax will likely gain importance. Some businesses may experience increased profits during the crisis, especially those embracing teleworking and digital commerce. Governments could incentivize investment while strengthening taxation on economic rents to boost resilience. The increased use of digital services and the need for revenue may accelerate international agreement on Pillar 1 issues.

Rising pressure on public finances may enhance the demand for effective minimum taxation of MNEs, ensuring a level playing field. Tax cooperation becomes crucial to avoid tax disputes escalating into trade wars, emphasizing the importance of progress in increasing tax certainty, dispute resolution, and prevention mechanisms. Increased revenue needs should drive investments in strengthened tax administrations through digitalization, benefiting compliance and reducing burdens. Simplifying taxation, including for micro businesses, can bring informal workers into the formal sector.

Looking Ahead to Domestic Resource Mobilization for Developing Countries

The COVID-19 crisis underscores global vulnerability, emphasizing the need for a collective effort in eradicating the virus and rebuilding economic life worldwide. While external financing is crucial in the short term, domestic resource mobilization, especially through taxation, remains the only long-term viable source of financing for public services, investment, and economic reconstruction.

Countries, particularly in Africa, need to increase their tax-to-GDP ratios by formalizing the economy, utilizing property and carbon taxes, and enhancing personal income tax performance. However, it is preferred to be more preoccupied with expanding the tax net instead of raising the tax burden of the already taxed. Building effective tax systems becomes critical for rebuilding the social-fiscal contract, fostering trust, and ensuring accountability between citizens and the state. The crisis provides an opportunity to assess changes in tax administration, leveraging digital technology for improved efficiency and increased revenues. International support for capacity development in tax administration and policy, led by the Platform for Collaboration on Tax, is essential.

As fiscal headroom tightens, developing countries' tolerance for international tax avoidance and evasion decreases. The time is ripe to assess the benefits low-income countries derive from international tax rules, address challenges, and ensure a fair distribution of reforms' direct benefits. The Inclusive Framework could lead a stock-taking exercise, focusing on country-by-country reporting and tax treaty abuse provisions, contributing to a new deal on international taxation in the post-COVID era.

Review Questions

1. How can targeted subsidies and deferrals of tax payments contribute to alleviating liquidity pressures for businesses during economic crises?

2. In what ways do social protection systems, such as short-time work schemes and unemployment benefits, stabilize households and support economic recovery?

3. What challenges do developing countries face in delivering rapid and effective support through their tax systems, especially considering large informal sectors?

4. How can stimulus measures be designed to ensure inclusivity, prevent windfall gains, and avoid long-term deficits?

5. What are the anticipated impacts of COVID-19 on global tax revenues, budget balances, and public debts, and how might countries address fiscal challenges?

6. Why is domestic resource mobilization, particularly through taxation,

considered crucial for long-term financing and economic reconstruction in developing countries?

Discussion Points

1. Policy Flexibility: Explore the balance between providing policy flexibility during crises and maintaining fiscal sustainability in the long term.
2. Global Cooperation: Discuss the importance of international collaboration in implementing effective stimulus measures and supporting developing countries.
3. Inclusive Recovery: Debate the challenges and strategies in ensuring an inclusive recovery, focusing on supporting vulnerable groups and addressing inequalities.

CHAPTER FIVE: FISCAL POLICY CHALLENGES IN THE EURO AREA: DEALING WITH HIGH INFLATION AND EXTERNAL SHOCKS

Summary of Key Points

1. Inflation Dynamics in the Euro Area: The Euro area experienced a significant and swift rise in inflation, reaching 10.6 percent in October 2022. This surge was primarily attributed to supply-side external shocks and internal demand-driven factors.

2. Impact on Public Finances: The intricate relationship between inflation and public finances depends on factors such as the nature and size of the inflation shock, fiscal responses, and monetary policy reactions. Higher inflation is traditionally expected to enhance public finances in the short term, but external shocks can reverse this positive impact.

3. Fiscal Policy Responses: Discretionary fiscal support increased in response to the energy and inflation shock, reaching nearly 2% of GDP in 2022 and 2023. However, there is uncertainty about the ultimate budget impact, with projections anticipating a withdrawal of fiscal support over 2024-25.

4. Automatic Adjustments to High Inflation: Approximately one-third of total government expenditure 2022 is automatically indexed to inflation,

particularly for pensions and wages. The inflation shock influences other government spending, even discretionary expenditures approved annually.

5. Budget Balance Impact: Studies indicate that the adverse effect on the euro area budget balance materializes one year after the inflation surge, resulting in a nearly 0.5 percent deterioration in the budget balance level in 2024. Longer-term simulations show similar conclusions.

6. Distributional Impact of Fiscal Measures: Governments implemented fiscal measures to mitigate the impact of inflation on households, particularly focusing on lower-income households. However, the distributional impact reveals that lower-income households still face a decline in purchasing power compared to higher-income households.

Fiscal Policy and High Inflation in the Euro Area

With the COVID-19 pandemic, the Euro area, like other advanced economies, had to grapple with challenges posed by a significant and swift rise in inflation. After nearly a decade below the European Central Bank's (ECB) 2 percent target, inflation surged from 1.9 percent in June 2021 to 10.6 percent in October 2022, dropping to 9.2 percent in December 2022. This spike is primarily attributed to supply-side external shocks and, to a lesser extent, internal demand-driven factors. The relationship between inflation and public finances is intricate and contingent on various factors. Traditionally, higher inflation is expected to enhance public finances, at least in the short term, due to increased government revenues, whereas public expenditure typically rises with a delay. However, the fiscal implications of an inflationary shock hinge on factors such as the nature and size of the inflation shock, fiscal responses, institutional aspects of government budgets, and monetary policy reactions. Furthermore, the fiscal policy response can influence the inflation outlook itself.

Inflation affects various components of public finances, including primary spending and revenues, market interest rates, public debt-to-GDP ratio, and the real value of debt. Traditionally, higher inflation has a positive, albeit relatively weak, impact on public finances in the short run. Empirical studies suggest that inflation can positively influence public finances if tax bases and collections adjust promptly and grow more than nominal GDP. However, when inflation is externally generated and reaches high levels, its positive impact on public finances can be reversed. Whether external or domestic, the nature of the inflation shock plays a crucial role in determining its effects on public finances. For instance, an external supply-side inflationary shock, such as a surge in imported energy prices, may have a more detrimental impact than a domestic shock.

How Inflation Affects Public Finances in the Euro Area

Significant discretionary fiscal support has been in response to the energy and inflation shock since 2020 and extending to 2023 following the Russia-Ukraine war. Fiscal support increased in 2022, reaching nearly 2% of GDP in 2022 and 2023. The ultimate budget impact depends on specific design, implementation, and market price developments. A substantial portion of the support is estimated to affect prices directly, with income measures making up the rest. Some countries have announced recalibration of measures to enhance targeting. The December 2022 Eurosystem projection anticipates a withdrawal of fiscal support over 2024-25, with a baseline of around 0.5 percent of GDP in 2024, reducing further to 0.2 percent in 2025. The size of these measures beyond this projection horizon depends on governments' fiscal decisions and energy price developments.

Automatic Adjustments of Public Finances to High Inflation: At the euro area aggregate level, approximately one-third of total government expenditure in 2022 is automatically indexed to inflation (75 percent), with the remainder mainly tied to wages (economy-wide wages, minimum wage). Notably, the indexation, particularly for pensions and wages, is predominantly backward-looking and lagged by a year. Public pensions constitute the largest share of total expenditure (21 percent), followed by unemployment benefits and other social benefits in cash (6 percent) and public wages (4 percent). "Other spending" (1 percent) mostly encompasses interest payments related to inflation-indexed debt. In addition to automatic indexation, an unanticipated increase in the prices of goods and services directly influences other government spending. Although nominal expenditures are approved annually in a discretionary manner within the budgetary process, an inflation shock, especially a substantial one, is likely to influence nominal public spending to some extent, even in the short run, which particularly applies to government purchases of goods and services and, to a certain extent, investment (which might be governed by longer-term contracts, potentially causing delays due to high inflation).

Estimated Impact of Inflation Surprise on Euro Area Budget Balance: Recent studies indicate that the adverse effect on the budget balance materializes one year after the inflation surge. In 2022, there is a broadly neutral overall effect. However, subsequent years witnessed intensified spending pressures that more than offset revenue benefits, resulting in nearly a 0.5 percent deterioration in the budget balance level in 2024. However, these results only partially reflect all the consequences of inflation and the monetary policy reaction, such as increased financing costs, revisions to real growth, or discretionary fiscal measures responding to high inflation. For longer-term effects, simulations of an inflationary external supply shock in a general equilibrium framework yield similar conclusions.

Stylized Simulations of Longer-Run Effects on Government Debt: Studies examining the implications of a stylized inflationary supply shock on the euro area's government debt outlook using a general equilibrium approach show that a negative impact on economic activity from an adverse external supply shock may outweigh the positive impact of higher inflation on debt ratios. In contrast, an internal demand shock would reduce the debt burden in the medium term. The analysis aims to illustrate the main propagation channels of a standardized external adverse shock to terms of trade, resembling certain features, but not the size, of the recent inflation increase.

Discretionary Fiscal Support for High Inflation: The fiscal support aimed at shielding the euro area economy from high inflation is estimated to have positive growth effects while reducing inflationary pressures during 2022-23. However, these effects are expected to be reversed over the rest of the projection horizon, primarily because the fiscal support in response to the energy shock is deemed temporary and, based on current policies, set to be mostly withdrawn by 2024. This support is projected to reduce inflation in 2022 and lower it in 2023. However, a reversal of the effect is anticipated in 2024 and 2025, leading to increased inflation persistence. The impact on HICP inflation mainly materializes through the energy component, with effects from higher demand following the fiscal stimulus building up more gradually.

Apart from energy and inflation support, other recent discretionary fiscal policy measures have smaller effects on growth and inflation over the projection horizon. Due to the timing and composition of these measures, positive impacts on growth are assessed to be present only in 2022, turning mildly negative in 2023 and more strongly negative over 2024-25 when a larger share of measures is withdrawn. The impact on inflation is less pronounced than the direct energy/inflation compensatory measures in the first two years of the projection horizon. Cumulatively, fiscal policy is estimated to positively impact euro area GDP and HICP, with a cumulative increase of about 2.3 percentage points and 0.8 percentage points, respectively, from 2020 to 2025 compared to a scenario of no fiscal policy change.

Distributional Impact of Fiscal Measures to Compensate for High Consumer Price Inflation: Governments across the euro area have undertaken substantial fiscal efforts to mitigate the impact of the current inflationary shock on households. Lower-income households, more affected by high consumer price inflation, have been the focus. However, the success of these measures in addressing the inflation gap has varied. On average, government measures have mitigated around one-quarter of the household income loss due to inflation in 2022. Price containment measures have temporarily lowered consumer prices, with estimates suggesting that consumer prices could have been about 1.7 percentage points higher without these measures. Simultaneously, income support measures contributed to increased nominal disposable income, compensating for around 60% of the 2022 rise in inflation. The distributional impact, however, reveals that lower-income households experiencing higher consumer inflation still face a decline in purchasing power compared to higher-income households. After considering both price and income measures, the remaining inflation gap between the highest and lowest quintiles is estimated to be around 1.2 percentage points.

While fiscal measures have been beneficial, especially for lower-income households, there is room for improvement in targeting and efficiency. Only a small portion of the support is estimated to reach lower-income households, and recalibrating measures could enhance both targeting and economic efficiency. Additionally, future adjustments should align with green transition goals and not discourage energy reduction efforts. Policymakers should carefully consider the long-term impact on public finances, especially in highly indebted countries, and balance the need for support with fiscal sustainability and economic incentives.

Alan Blinder's Perspectives on Monetary vs Fiscal Policy

Alan Blinder, known for his insightful and balanced macroeconomic policy analysis, has devoted much of his career to teaching at Princeton. He has also served as a president of the President's Council of Economic Advisers under Clinton and vice-chair of the Federal Reserve, providing policy guidance during Alan Greenspan's tenure. Blinder's influence extends beyond his academic contributions, as he has authored numerous technical and popular books addressing topics from globalization to the 2008 financial crisis. His prolific writing includes hundreds of opinion columns in the Wall Street Journal, showcasing his ability to communicate complex ideas effectively. In his latest work, "A Monetary and Fiscal History of the United States, 1961-2022," Blinder weaves a narrative that aims to explain the dynamic interplay between monetary and fiscal policy over the six decades 1961-2021, wherein the shifts in economic thought and policymaking strategies are thoroughly explored, laboriously highlighting the evolution of attitudes toward monetary and fiscal policy.

Theoretical Frameworks for Public Finance and Fiscal Policy

Understanding public finance and fiscal policy relies on various theoretical frameworks, each offering distinct perspectives on the government's role in the economy, the impact of taxation and spending, and optimal strategies for economic objectives. Here are key theoretical frameworks:

1. Classical Economics: Rooted in Adam Smith and David Ricardo's ideas, classical economics emphasizes free markets and minimal government intervention. Advocates for a laissez-faire approach, limiting government involvement to ensuring property rights and contract enforcement.

2. Keynesian Economics: Developed by John Maynard Keynes during the Great Depression, it advocated active government intervention to manage aggregate demand and stabilize the economy. Recommends expansionary fiscal policies during downturns and contractionary measures during periods of inflation.

3. Monetarism: Associated with Milton Friedman, monetarism focuses on the money supply's role in economic outcomes. Advocates stable monetary policy, often skeptical of fiscal policy, emphasizing inflation control through monetary measures.

4. New Classical Economics: Building on classical principles, it assumes individuals have rational expectations and adjust behavior based on anticipated policy changes. Questions the effectiveness of discretionary fiscal policies, suggesting individuals will offset government actions.

5. New Keynesian Economics: Extends Keynesian ideas, incorporating microeconomic foundations and market imperfections. Advocates targeted government interventions, such as fiscal stimulus during recessions, emphasizing the importance of both monetary and fiscal policy.

6. Public Choice Theory: Applies economic analysis to political behavior, assuming individuals act in self-interest. Highlights how political actors may pursue policies benefiting specific interests over broader public welfare.

7. Institutional Economics: Associated with scholars like Douglass North, it focuses on how institutions impact economic behavior. Emphasizes the role of institutions in shaping fiscal policies and analyzes their influence on fiscal institutions, tax systems, and public spending programs.

These frameworks provide diverse perspectives on the government's role and fiscal policy design. Policymakers often integrate elements from multiple frameworks to address complex economic challenges.

The Rise and Fall of Keynesianism: Keynesian economics and its rise and fall constitute another significant theme. While Friedman and Schwartz, prominent monetarists, rejected Keynesianism, Blinder elucidates how Keynesianism experienced cycles of ascendancy and decline, influencing both economic theory and policy decisions. The role of budget deficits takes center stage in discussions about fiscal policy over his 60-year study period. Blinder outlines revolutionary changes in perceptions of budget deficits, noting a transformation from viewing them as dangerous or immoral at the beginning of the covered period to accepting them as necessary or even beneficial by the end.

Central Bank Independence: A less-explored theme is central bank independence, which has become a cornerstone of effective monetary policy. Blinder sheds light on how attitudes toward central bank independence shifted from being questioned and debated in 1961 to being widely accepted as a pillar of sound monetary policy in later years. He poses a crucial question about leadership in formulating and executing stabilization policy: Should it be the central bank or the fiscal authorities? He examines the implications of this choice on various macroeconomic variables, highlighting the significance of both monetary and fiscal policy in shaping economic outcomes.

The historical context before 1961 saw neither fiscal nor monetary policy deliberately aimed at managing aggregate demand. Blinder underscores how this changed significantly with President Kennedy's deliberate use of discretionary fiscal policy to influence aggregate demand through tax cuts in 1962, marking a departure from prior approaches. The narrative continues with Reagan's era, where fiscal policy made a strong comeback, challenging the notion that it could be ignored. However, Blinder observes that the focus shifted from stimulating the economy to reducing the budget deficit, with monetary policy taking the lead in managing demand. Blinder's book also delves into the Clinton administration's unique approach to fiscal policy, emphasizing deficit reduction through tax increases and spending cuts, acknowledging the success of this strategy and defying expectations that a sizable fiscal contraction would slow the economy.

Perspectives on the 2008 Financial Crisis: Blinder explores the 2008 financial crisis, contrasting monetary and fiscal policy roles. The Federal Reserve, under Ben Bernanke, took the lead in responding to the crisis, employing aggressive interest rate cuts. Fiscal policy played a supporting role, with modest tax cuts passed by the Bush administration. The narrative shifts to President Obama's term, where fiscal policy briefly regained prominence with a large stimulus package but was constrained by a divided Congress. Monetary policy once again assumed a more dominant role in the absence of substantial fiscal support. Blinder critically analyzes the post-2009 period, highlighting the erratic nature of fiscal policy and its shift to contractionary measures during 2011-2013, which, coupled with the reduced potency of monetary policy, contributed to a slow economic recovery.

The COVID-19 Pandemic: The final chapter of Blinder's historical account revolves around the Covid-19 pandemic. Both monetary and fiscal policy assumed a central role in responding to the economic fallout. The Federal Reserve implemented various measures, and Congress passed substantial relief packages, showcasing the necessity of coordinated policy responses during unprecedented crises.

Reflecting on the 60-year trajectory, Blinder concludes that the arc of history slightly favored monetary policy in 2021, with economists and policy-makers turning more towards the Federal Reserve than Congress. However, he emphasizes that this trend is minor compared to the notable cycles and shifts in fiscal and monetary policy roles over the decades. Blinder's comprehensive exploration of the complex dynamics between monetary and fiscal policy offers valuable insights into the evolving landscape of macroeconomic policymaking in the United States.

Challenges in Fiscal Policy Implementation

Political Considerations: Fiscal policy decisions often reflect partisan divides, leading to gridlock or policies prioritizing short-term political gains over long-term stability. Policymakers need help to balance immediate results with long-term sustainability, potentially sacrificing long-term goals for short-term gains during electoral cycles.

Institutional Constraints: Bureaucratic hurdles - inefficiencies, red tape, and resistance to change - can impede policy implementation, especially in developing countries facing bureaucratic challenges. Legal and regulatory challenges posed by complex tax codes, overlapping jurisdictions, and legal disputes may hinder fiscal policy implementation, as seen in the European Union's challenges in coordinating fiscal policies.

Cases and Examples

1. U.S. Government Shutdowns: Political disagreements lead to government shutdowns, impacting economic stability and highlighting challenges in reaching bipartisan fiscal agreements.
2. Greek Debt Crisis and Austerity Measures: Implementing austerity measures during the Greek debt crisis faces political and social backlash, emphasizing the difficulty of balancing economic challenges and political resistance.
3. Bureaucratic Challenges in India's Tax Reforms: India's tax reforms, including the Goods and Services Tax (GST), face bureaucratic hurdles, showcasing how administrative challenges affect fiscal policy execution.

Addressing these challenges requires policymakers to navigate political and institutional complexities for effective fiscal policy design and implementation.

Contemporary Issues in Fiscal Policy and Taxation

Challenges

Cross-Border Taxation

1. Double Taxation Treaties: Agreements between countries, such as the U.S.-Canada Tax Treaty, address double taxation issues and promote cross-border investment and trade.
2. Transfer Pricing Issues: Guidelines developed by the OECD address mispricing in transactions between multinational entities, ensuring fair taxation and curbing profit shifting.

Fiscal Coordination in Regional Blocks

1. European Union Fiscal Policies: Despite challenges, the EU aims for fiscal coordination among member states, as seen in the Stability and Growth Pact, highlighting ongoing efforts to enhance coordination.
2. ASEAN Economic Community Perspectives: ASEAN's goal of economic integration faces challenges due to varying economic conditions and fiscal policies among member states, necessitating ongoing efforts for greater fiscal coordination.

Cases and Examples

1. Base Erosion and Profit Shifting (BEPS): The OECD's BEPS project addresses tax planning strategies used by multinational enterprises, requiring international cooperation for effective implementation.
2. European Debt Crisis and Fiscal Challenges: The Eurozone crisis exposes weak fiscal coordination among EU states, emphasizing the need for closer fiscal integration to prevent imbalances and crises.
3. ASEAN's Varied Fiscal Policies: Diverse fiscal policies among ASEAN member states reflect variations in economic structures, complicating efforts to achieve greater fiscal coordination.

Addressing these challenges requires collaborative efforts among nations and regional organizations to balance national interests and international cooperation in fiscal matters.

Innovations

Digital Economy and Tax Challenges

1. Taxing E-commerce and Digital Transactions: The digital economy challenges traditional tax systems, leading to initiatives like the OECD's BEPS project and digital services taxes to ensure fair taxation.
2. Global Efforts for Digital Taxation: Global frameworks, such as the OECD's Pillar One and Pillar Two proposals, aim to reform international taxation, addressing complexities in taxing multinational tech companies.

Environmental Taxation

1. Carbon Taxes and Cap-and-Trade Systems: Environmental taxation strategies, like the EU ETS, incentivize emission reductions by internalizing the social cost of carbon.
2. Incentivizing Green Practices: Governments use tax incentives to promote environmentally friendly practices, such as tax credits for renewable energy projects and aligning taxation with environmental goals.

Cases and Examples

1. Digital Services Taxes in Europe: European countries implement digital services taxes to address the under-taxation of digital giants, leading to trade tensions and illustrating challenges in a globally interconnected digital economy.
2. Global Minimum Corporate Tax Agreement: G20 finance ministers endorse a global minimum corporate tax rate to prevent tax avoidance,

showcasing international efforts to address profit shifting and ensure fair taxation.

3. Plastic Tax in the European Union: To address plastic waste, the EU is considering a plastic tax to encourage sustainable practices and discourage single-use plastics.

4. Addressing contemporary issues involves designing effective tax policies in response to the changing nature of economic activities and global environmental challenges, balancing economic growth with concerns like digital taxation and environmental sustainability.

Review Questions

1. What factors contributed to the significant rise in inflation in the Euro area, and how did it impact public finances?

2. How does the nature of an inflation shock, whether external or domestic, influence its effects on government budgets and public finances?

3. What is the estimated impact of fiscal support on inflation in the Euro area over the projection horizon of 2022-2025?

4. Explain the automatic adjustments of public finances to high inflation and their implications for different components of government spending.

5. How do studies project the budget balance impact of inflation in the Euro area, and what are the key factors considered in these projections?

6. Evaluate the distributional impact of fiscal measures on households in the Euro area facing high consumer price inflation.

Discussion Points

1. Long-Term Fiscal Sustainability: How can policymakers balance fiscal support in response to external shocks with long-term fiscal sustainability, especially in highly indebted countries?

2. Role of Monetary Policy: How does monetary policy interact with fiscal

policy during periods of high inflation, and how can coordinated efforts be optimized for economic stability?

3. Green Transition Goals: Considering the distributional impact of fiscal measures, how can future adjustments align with green transition goals and ensure they do not discourage efforts toward energy reduction?

CHAPTER SIX: INFLATION MANAGEMENT, FISCAL POLITICS AND TAX TREATIES

Summary of Key Points

1. Inflation's Distributive Effects:

   - Unexpected inflation favors debtors over bondholders, particularly in countries with debt exceeding 50% of GDP.
   - Each percentage point of unexpected inflation reduces public debt by 0.6 percentage points of GDP for several years.

2. Household Impact of Inflation:

   - Inflation affects households through consumption patterns, income sources, and assets/liabilities.
   - Rising food prices disproportionately impact lower-income families.
   - Wealth redistribution occurs based on age groups.

3. Fiscal Policy and Inflation Management:

   - Statistical evidence suggests that reducing public expenditure by 1% of GDP in advanced economies has lowered inflation by 0.5% since 1985.

- Fiscal policy is crucial for managing inflation and supporting vulnerable populations.

4. Fiscal Policy's Growth Channels:

- Endorses endogenous growth theory to analyze the long-term impact of fiscal policy on growth.
- Fiscal reforms can lift medium- to long-term growth by ¾ of a percentage point in advanced economies.
- Identifies macro and structural tax and expenditure policies as the main growth channels.

5. Equity Implications of Fiscal Reforms:

- Departure from other studies by explicitly considering equity implications of fiscal policy reforms.
- Highlights the importance of balancing efficiency and equity objectives for public support.

6. Political Dynamics in Fiscal Policymaking:

- Schumpeter's view on the interdependence of economic, social, and political processes in fiscal politics.
- Elections influence economic policies, leading to macroeconomic unpredictability.
- Fiscal policies are inherently political, involving a struggle for political power and shaping income distribution.

Fiscal Policy and Inflation Management

Addressing inflation and safeguarding vulnerable populations are critical tasks for policymakers. In their April 3, 2023, article, Vitor Gaspar, Carlos Eduardo Goncalves, Paolo Mauro, and Marcos Poplawski-Ribeiro delve into the complexities of inflation's distributive effects and propose strategies for effective fiscal policy. The authors stress the importance of comprehending how inflation impacts diverse segments of society during a significant inflationary surge. To achieve this understanding, they analyzed the period from mid-2021 to mid-2022, focusing on the rise in food and energy prices. They found that unexpected inflation diminishes the real value of government debt, favoring debtors over bondholders. This effect is particularly pronounced for countries with debt exceeding 50% of GDP. The study indicates that each percentage point of unexpected inflation reduces public debt by 0.6 percentage points of GDP for several years.

Drawing from public surveys across six economies, the authors highlight three main channels through which inflation affects households: consumption patterns, income sources (wages, pensions, transfers), and assets/liabilities. Notable findings include the disproportionate impact of rising food prices on lower-income families and the redistributive wealth effects based on age groups. The authors assert that fiscal policy is crucial in managing inflation and supporting vulnerable populations. They present statistical evidence suggesting that, since 1985, reducing public expenditure by 1 percent of GDP in advanced economies has lowered inflation by 0.5 percent. Additionally, fiscal policy can protect the vulnerable by providing targeted support. The authors focus on the broader implications of fiscal policy on medium- to long-term growth. Fiscal policy, they argue, is a potent tool that can positively impact growth through various channels. They stress the need for a balanced approach tailored to country-specific conditions.

Key Observations

1. Endogenous Growth Theory: The analysis employs endogenous growth theory, differentiating it from neoclassical growth theory. This framework enables studying how government policy can affect long-term growth, emphasizing the challenge of distinguishing permanent and transitory effects.

2. Fiscal Reforms and Growth: Drawing on extensive technical assistance and country studies, the authors find that fiscal reforms can lift medium-

to long-term growth by ¾ of a percentage point in advanced economies and potentially more in developing economies.

3. Growth Channels: The paper identifies macro and structural tax and expenditure policies as the main growth channels. It emphasizes the role of fiscal policy in ensuring macroeconomic stability, promoting human capital accumulation, and boosting employment, investment, and productivity.

4. Equity Implications: In a departure from other studies, this paper explicitly considers the equity implications of fiscal policy reforms. It highlights the importance of fostering public support through social dialogue and balancing efficiency and equity objectives.

In summary, the authors underscore the substantial growth dividends that fiscal reforms can yield. They emphasize the need for a comprehensive, internally consistent approach combining fiscal and complementary structural reforms. They argue that the success of these reforms is contingent on effective policy design, social consensus, and a careful balance between growth and equity objectives.

Fiscal Stimulus Effects and Potential Offsetting Factors

A Fiscal policy serves as a mechanism through which the government manipulates its spending and revenue to influence the overall economy, involving adjusting government spending and tax revenue levels to impact economic activity in the short term. When the government incurs a budget deficit, it generates fiscal stimulus, boosting economic activity. Conversely, a budget surplus signifies fiscal contraction, slowing economic activity. Expansionary fiscal policy aims to stimulate economic activity during a recession. The government achieves this by increasing spending, reducing tax revenue, or combining both strategies. Increased government spending directly influences economic activity by purchasing goods and services from the private sector. At the same time, reduced tax revenue indirectly boosts economic activity by raising individuals' disposable income, leading to increased spending.

Expansionary fiscal policy is beneficial during a recession, mitigating negative impacts like high unemployment and stagnant wages. However, its application during economic expansions can lead to rising interest rates, growing trade deficits, and accelerating inflation, partially offsetting its positive effects. In contrast, contractionary fiscal policy aims to slow economic activity, which is achieved by decreasing government spending, increasing tax revenue, or combining both. Reduced government spending directly affects economic activity by limiting purchases from the private sector, while increased tax revenue lowers individuals' disposable income, reducing spending on goods and services. Policymakers may choose to reduce fiscal stimulus as the economy exits a recession to avoid negative consequences. Historically, the federal government has followed a pattern of increasing fiscal stimulus during recessions and decreasing it during economic recovery.

During a recession, fiscal stimulus, achieved through increased spending or reduced tax revenue, can lead to higher interest rates, reducing investment and consumer spending. This phenomenon, known as crowding out, is influenced by the economy's position in the business cycle. The government can also influence the economy through monetary policy executed by the Federal Reserve. Adjusting interest rates can complement fiscal policy or offset its effects. Fiscal expansion multipliers, which measure the impact of fiscal stimulus, vary based on the form of stimulus.

Long-Term Considerations and Risks: Persistently applying fiscal stimulus has potential drawbacks. It can contribute to a rising debt-to-GDP ratio, limiting economic growth and requiring more budget allocation to interest payments. Some research suggests a negative impact of high public debt on economic growth. As the economy improves, policymakers may withdraw fiscal stimulus by reducing the deficit or applying contractionary fiscal policy, mitigating negative consequences like decreasing investment, rising trade deficits, and accelerating inflation. The impact of withdrawing fiscal stimulus depends on factors such as interest rates, trade balances, and inflation. Striking a balance between stimulating economic growth and managing long-term risks is essential for sustainable economic development. Fiscal policy decisions should be informed by the economy's current state and potential impacts on interest rates, trade balances, inflation, and overall economic stability.

Fiscal Politics and Management of the Economy

"Fiscal Politics underlies the dynamics of fiscal policymaking in political economy, which views economic, social, and political processes as interdependent and co-evolutionary. In a seminal work, 'Capitalism, Socialism and Democracy' (1942), Schumpeter defines democratic regimes as institutions that give rise to a struggle for political power—a competition to secure the people's vote and the right to wield that power. This perspective influenced subsequent political economists, including Downs (1957), who characterized electoral politics as a battle for the median voter. In particular, Schumpeter's concept of the modern tax state highlights a tension between the state's involvement in social and political dynamics and the necessity for private and civil spheres to develop independently. According to Schumpeter, public finances transcend narrow economic considerations, as reflected in his assertion that "The spirit of a people, its cultural level, its social structure, the deeds its policy may prepare—all this and more is written in its fiscal history" (Schumpeter, 1991, p. 101). In fiscal politics, it is argued that modern states require both economic and political capabilities, which are deeply intertwined; economic performance influences the ability of incumbent governments to implement their policies, impacting their electoral prospects.

The Power of Elections: Even during periods of political stability, electoral outcomes, and polarization can shape economic policies and the state of the economy. Different political parties pursue distinct economic goals, contributing to macroeconomic unpredictability. The consciousness of election outcomes has an impact on budgetary policies and the expenditure preferences of the government. There is a strong association between political fragmentation, fiscal discipline, and the dominant political ideology, and politically determined fiscal rules and institutions strongly influence fiscal outcomes. Accordingly, politics, whether at the national or supranational level, plays a crucial role in fiscal policymaking. Thus, understanding the dominant political dynamics is vital, especially when facing challenges in implementing growth-friendly fiscal policies post-financial meltdown.

How Politics Shapes Fiscal Policy

Fiscal policy, commonly described as "the matter of who gets what, when, and how," is profoundly influenced by political considerations. The core functions of a typical government—allocation, distribution, and stabilization—are inherently political. Politics directly impacts the provision of public goods, especially concerning stabilization and redistributive policies. For instance, when a government runs a fiscal deficit to stabilize the economy, it involves a political decision with intergenerational implications. Discussions in the parliament about revenue and expenditure composition are outcomes of political bargaining that affect income distribution and may lead to unintended economic consequences.

The study of fiscal politics dates back to the nineteenth century, with the Italian and Swedish schools analyzing how governments make policy choices. Throughout the twentieth century, the Public Choice school focused on political incentives and constraints in policy formulation, with scholars like Buchanan (1960) stressing voters' inability to comprehend fiscal intricacies. His revived interest in political determinants of fiscal policy led to various models examining factors such as electoral systems, fiscal centralization, and budgetary laws. These models provided a framework for empirically testing the impact of political factors on fiscal decisions.

Recent political economy models attempt to explain deviations from the tax-smoothing framework, which posits that public debt results from optimal fiscal policy smoothing tax rates over time. These political and economic models attribute observed deficits and public debt fluctuations to institutional factors mediated by electoral constraints. Although these models vary with electoral systems, fiscal centralization, and budgetary laws, their primary contribution provides the foundational framework for empirically testing the influence of political factors on fiscal economic decisions. Three sets of factors have consistently been identified as influencing fiscal policies: (1) election timing, allowing voters to reward or punish the government for economic policies; (2) the ideology of the governing party regarding the state's size and role in the economy; and (3) political fragmentation, determining the number of actors involved in fiscal policy decisions.

Impact of Election Timing: Elections primarily affect the government's stabilization and redistribution functions. The proximity of elections can influence budget decisions in various ways. Firstly, if the government believes economic growth improves its reelection chances, it may opt for a fiscal expansion before elections, leading to political budget cycles. However, if this is not compensated during the incumbent's tenure, it results in debt accumulation from one political cycle to the next. This bias relies on assumptions of fiscal illusion among voters and voter ignorance about budget details and long-term impacts. A second electoral effect involves the strategic use of debt by the incumbent government. For instance, a conservative government anticipating a leftist successor may strategically leave less funds, tying the hands of the incoming government and increasing its chances of electoral defeat in the next cycle. This behavior is more intense in younger democracies and less transparent systems, contributing to delayed fiscal adjustments.

Ideology of the Cabinet: The governing party's ideology influences its policy agenda and the goal of remaining in office. Ideology surfaces in tax-and-spend policies related to redistribution and can also impact decisions on macroeconomic stabilization. Left-wing governments are associated with expansionary fiscal policies to address unemployment, while right-wing governments prioritize inflation concerns, leading to different budgetary approaches. For instance, left-wing governments focus on interventionist supply-side policies, particularly public investment, fostering higher growth rates. Ideology significantly shapes fiscal policies related to redistribution. Left-wing parties, supported by workers and low- to middle-income populations, emphasize income inequality, social benefits, and progressive taxation. In contrast, right-wing governments favor a smaller role for the government, supporting a stronger private sector. Backed by economically stronger segments, right-wing parties tend to tax and spend less than their left-wing counterparts.

While the cabinet's ideology is a crucial predictor of fiscal policy, its role may vary, especially when the government's credibility is at stake. Cabinets may signal commitment and gain credibility by pursuing fiscal adjustments against the preferences of their constituents. The influence of ideology on government actions may also vary depending on the development of the underlying welfare state. Thus, understanding the intricate relationship between politics and fiscal policy involves examining factors such as election timing, ideological leanings of the governing party, and political fragmentation. This book contributes to unraveling these complexities and emphasizes the need for adapting fiscal policy advice to evolving political and economic landscapes."

Executive vs Legislature Politics: The impact of politics on the provision of public goods is particularly relevant in stabilization and redistributive policies. For instance, when the executive branch runs a fiscal deficit to stabilize the economy, it entails a political decision with intergenerational implications. Additionally, discussions in the parliament about revenue and expenditure composition are outcomes of political bargaining, affecting income distribution and potentially leading to unintended economic consequences.

Political Fragmentation: Political fragmentation, reflected in decision-making diversity, is detrimental to expenditure control and fiscal discipline. It affects the government's three functions, leading to difficulties in achieving consensus on balanced budgets. The "common pool problem" suggests that multiple parties with different ideologies struggle to agree on spending programs, resulting in deviations from optimal fiscal policy. More actors in fiscal decision-making intensify expenditure pressure, deviating further from optimal fiscal policy, which affects the government's stabilization function, leading to delays in fiscal consolidation, especially in coalition governments or cabinets with numerous spending ministries. Studies confirm that fragmented governments are associated with larger public deficits, and the presence of many veto players makes spending cuts challenging to implement. As veto players increase, fiscal adjustment becomes slower, leading to suboptimal public debt accumulation.

Mitigating Political Influence on Fiscal Policy

Various approaches have been attempted to mitigate the influence of political factors on fiscal policy. One primary response involves introducing fiscal rules and frameworks to limit politicians' budgetary discretion. The effectiveness of these institutions, however, remains to be mixed. Fiscal rules, introduced in many countries since the 1990s, aim to prevent conflicts in fiscal policy due to special interests. Well-designed rules should be clear, simple, transparent, consistent, flexible, and enforceable. On average, countries with fiscal rules exhibit improved fiscal performance, with rules associated with less procyclical policies. However, the positive association may reflect changing attitudes toward fiscal rectitude rather than a direct impact of the rules on fiscal outcomes. Additionally, fiscal frameworks focused on transparent and credible strategies can support fiscal discipline.

Fiscal institutions, especially in the presence of ideological fragmentation, play a crucial role in fiscal policy. Comprehensive fiscal reporting, forecasting, and risk disclosure contribute to more sustainable public finances. Strengthening budget institutions, performance budgeting systems, and intergovernmental fiscal arrangements can enhance the implementation of budget plans. Developing countries, especially those reliant on natural resources, benefit from strengthening fiscal institutions to resist political pressures to overspend. Independent fiscal councils have been introduced to provide unbiased information and analysis and monitor compliance with fiscal rules. Well-designed fiscal councils, with strict operational independence, public assessment of budget forecasts, and a strong presence in public debate, can promote stronger fiscal discipline.

Tax Treaties Between Countries

A tax treaty, also known as a Double Tax Agreement (DTA), is a bilateral agreement between two countries to resolve issues related to the double taxation of their respective citizens' passive and active income. These treaties, which determine the amount of tax applicable to income, capital, estate, or wealth, play a crucial role in international tax relations. The key points of a typical tax treaty are the following:

1. Tax treaties are agreements between two countries to address double taxation of their citizens' income.
2. These treaties determine the tax amount a country can apply to various types of income.
3. Tax havens, often countries with low or no corporate taxes, typically do not enter into tax treaties.

When individuals or businesses invest in a foreign country, the question arises of which country should tax the investor's earnings. The source country (hosting the investment) and the residence country (investor's country) may enter into a tax treaty to avoid double taxation. The source country may also be called the capital-importing country, while the residence country may be called the capital-exporting country.

Two prevalent models for tax treaties are the Organization for Economic Co-operation and Development (OECD) Model and the United Nations (UN) Model Convention. The OECD Model is more favorable to capital-exporting countries, requiring the source country to give up some or all of its tax on certain income categories earned by residents of the other treaty country. On the other hand, the UN Model favors the foreign country of investment, particularly benefiting developing countries. The OECD Model favors capital-exporting countries, while the UN Model is more favorable to foreign investment countries.

Withholding Taxes Policy: A critical aspect of tax treaties is their policy on withholding taxes, which determines the tax levied on income (such as interest and dividends) non-residents earn. For example, if a tax treaty establishes a bilateral withholding tax on dividends at 10%, the source country taxes dividend payments to the other country at that rate. The U.S., for instance, has tax treaties with various countries to reduce or eliminate taxes paid by foreign residents. These treaties are reciprocal, applying to both treaty countries. However, for individuals residing in countries without tax treaties with the U.S., any U.S.-earned income is taxed according to standard U.S. rates.

Common Challenges with Operational Transfer Pricing (OTP): Implementing Transfer Pricing policies poses challenges for businesses, regardless of scale or complexity. Operational Transfer Pricing (OTP), focusing on policy implementation, involves data, processes, people, and technology. The challenges and considerations are summarized below:

1. Unreliable Data: Extracting and ensuring the right level of granularity in data can take time and effort. Standardizing source data and implementing appropriate governance is essential for accuracy and consistency.
2. Non-Standardization of Calculations: Manual processes and legacy Excel spreadsheets can lead to errors. Standardizing and automating processes can reduce risks and save time.
3. Key Person Risk: Relying on specific individuals for OTP processes poses a challenge. Developing process documentation and providing training can mitigate this risk.
4. Poor Risk Management and Controls: Lack of a governance framework can lead to overlooked risks. A clear risk strategy, controls, and documentation are essential for effective risk management.
5. Choosing the Right Technology: Reliance on Excel spreadsheets may need more controls. Choosing appropriate technology tools and considering specific requirements is critical for successful OTP implementation.

Understanding tax treaties and addressing operational transfer pricing challenges is crucial for businesses engaged in international transactions. Clear policies, effective implementation, and adherence to international standards contribute to successful cross-border financial management.

Addressing Transfer Pricing Challenges: Lessons from Vietnam

Foreign Direct Investment (FDI) companies are pivotal in Vietnam's economic development, contributing significantly to job creation and improved living standards. However, the Vietnamese tax authorities have identified transfer pricing (TP) and tax evasion issues among these entities, increasing efforts to enhance tax administration and governance. Historical data indicates that around 50 percent of FDI companies in Vietnam reported losses for consecutive financial years, particularly in sectors such as garment and footwear processing, which raised concerns as similar domestic companies in these industries were profitable. Notable examples, including Coca-Cola Beverages Vietnam Ltd., prompted heightened scrutiny.

Increased Focus by Tax Authorities: Vietnamese tax authorities have intensified their focus on TP issues during audits, transitioning from specialized TP teams to a national-scale approach. Recent audit sessions involve extensive information requests, real-time data scrutiny, and thorough interviews with key personnel, reflecting a shift toward a more comprehensive examination.

Importance of Timely TP Documentation: Timely preparation of TP compliance documentation is critical. Decree 132/2020/ND-CP mandates annual TP documentation preparation before submitting a company's annual Corporate Income Tax (CIT) return. While not mandatory for submission, CIT returns must include TP Appendices covering related-party information, local and master file checklists, and information disclosure on national profit.

Challenges in TP Compliance Documentation: Companies often face challenges in TP compliance due to:

1. Late Preparation: Some companies should pay attention to TP compliance until external auditors or tax advisors raise concerns, underestimating the importance of timely documentation.
2. Backdating Dossiers: Instances where TP dossiers are backdated to align with CIT return lodgment yet rejected by tax authorities due to inconsistencies with engagement dates.
3. Inconsistencies in Appendices: Discrepancies in reporting related-party

transactions between TP Appendices and TP documentation, leading to rejection by tax auditing teams.

4. Loss-Making Companies: Tax authorities scrutinize entities with continuous losses, questioning their going-concern status and considering whether other affiliated entities within international groups should bear losses.

5. Low Profitability: Companies underestimating the importance of benchmarking their performance may face challenges. Tax authorities expect consistent profitability, especially in cost-centered entities, and may question low-profit results.

6. Arm's Length Range Compliance: The arm's length range, now from the 35th to the 75th percentile, requires companies to substantiate their profitability within this range, necessitating economic analyses.

To navigate the evolving landscape of TP compliance in Vietnam, companies must prioritize timely documentation, address inconsistencies, and proactively manage challenges related to loss-making entities and low profitability. Adherence to regulations and comprehensive economic analyses are essential for sustaining business operations and mitigating tax-related risks.

Review Questions

1. How does unexpected inflation impact the distribution of wealth between debtors and bondholders?

2. According to the authors, What are the three main channels through which inflation affects households?

3. How has fiscal policy lowered inflation in advanced economies since 1985?

4. Explain the role of fiscal reforms in promoting medium- to long-term growth, according to the authors.

5. What is the significance of considering equity implications in fiscal policy reforms, and how does it differ from other studies?

6. How do elections influence fiscal policies, and how does political ideology shape fiscal approaches?

Discussion Points

1. Policy Design for Vulnerable Populations: · Explore strategies for designing fiscal policies that effectively support vulnerable populations during inflationary periods.
2. Balancing Efficiency and Equity: Discuss the challenges and benefits of balancing efficiency and equity objectives in fiscal reforms.
3. Global Implications of Fiscal Policy: Explore how the principles and findings discussed in the text can be applied or adapted in different global economic contexts.

CHAPTER SEVEN: CHAPTER SEVEN: MEANING AND APPLICATION OF IMPLEMENTATION ANALYSIS

Summary of Key Points

1. Introduction to Implementation Analysis: Despite predictable implementation issues in government programs, there is a tendency for legislators to overlook them during program enactment. Implementation Analysis, facilitated by the Government Accountability Office (GAO), is proposed for major legislative proposals in the United States, drawing inspiration from the Congressional Budget Office's budget scoring experience.

2. Scope of Implementation Analysis: Implementation Analysis focuses on national and sectoral contexts, aiming to anticipate and address potential issues before policy enactment. It emphasizes the need for sustained attention and a standardized methodology to identify and resolve ambiguities in legislation, potential conflicts with organizational missions, and coordination challenges among implementing agencies.

3. Challenges and Benefits of Implementation Analysis: Despite political and administrative challenges, Implementation Analysis offers a valuable framework for anticipating and addressing implementation problems. A checklist of standards and concerns contributes to informed decision-making during the policymaking process, ensuring better government performance and achieving policy objectives.

4. Resource and Organizational Capacity Constraints: Politicians often prioritize objectives, overlooking implementation challenges. Implementation Analysis focuses on organizational capacity and resource flow, assessing the stock and flow of necessary resources compared with legislative proposals to ensure realistic program expectations.

5. Target Compliance Challenges in Policy Implementation: Even when resource constraints and front-line worker behavior are managed, the intended targets of government policies may not behave as anticipated. Implementation Analysis identifies challenges such as insufficient incentives, behavioral biases, poor monitoring, information gaps, and target hostility, demanding distinct strategic responses.

6. Framework for Implementation Analysis: The Implementation Analysis process involves analyzing tasks, comparing them with a checklist, gathering preliminary evidence, conducting a detailed analysis, and publishing a comprehensive report with potential strategic responses. It provides key considerations for addressing analytical issues, organizational overload concerns, timeline issues, and overall effectiveness.

Enhancing Government's Implementation Analysis

Government programs often need help in achieving policy objectives due to implementation issues. The negative impact of these problems extends to agency morale and public perception. Despite the predictability of many implementation problems, legislators tend to overlook them during program enactment. Hence, there is a need for the adoption of Implementation Analysis for major legislative proposals in the United States, facilitated by the Government Accountability Office (GAO), drawing inspiration from the Congressional Budget Office's budget scoring experience. Anticipating implementation problems is crucial, spanning sectors like homeland security, health care, welfare reform, and climate change. The literature on policy implementation highlights the importance of addressing potential issues before a policy is enacted. However, there needs to be more sustained attention and a standardized methodology for such analysis, partly due to the absence of incentives for politicians to identify problems during the legislative process.

Implementation Analysis requires a focus on national and sectoral contexts. Ambiguities in legislation, especially key indeterminacies, can lead to interpretation issues. While some degree of ambiguity may be beneficial, Implementation Analysis aims to identify areas with substantial vagueness, enabling legislators to decide whether to address these ambiguities. Organizations develop distinctive cultures and missions over time, shaping their behavior and minimizing communication costs. When new tasks conflict with an organization's established mission, a learning curve or resistance may arise. Implementation Analysis aims to identify potential conflicts between established organizational missions and new tasks, guiding policymakers on whether to create new implementing agencies or adapt existing ones.

Though facing political and administrative challenges, Implementation Analysis offers a valuable framework for anticipating and addressing implementation problems. A checklist of standards and concerns can significantly contribute to informed decision-making during the policymaking process. Identifying potential pitfalls early on ensures better government performance and the achievement of policy objectives. Reform proposals often demand collaboration among existing organizations, but protection of interests, jobs, and constituencies may hinder efficient administration. Poor coordination mechanisms among implementing agencies lead to service breakdowns, delays, bureaucratic hurdles, and cost overruns. Implementation Analysis can dissect the "supply chain" of program decisions, identify potential cooperation challenges, and propose strategies to enhance inter-agency coordination without compromising specialization.

Resource and Organizational Capacity Constraints: Politicians prioritize objectives, often overlooking implementation challenges and resisting resource allocations. A dual focus on organizational capacity and resource flow is essential. Organizational capacity involves acquiring and retaining expertise, equipment, and reputation, while resource flow pertains to short-term funding and program inputs. Implementation Analysis assesses the stock and flow of necessary resources, comparing it with legislative proposals, ensuring realistic program expectations.

Timeline Issues: Regarding resource constraints, timelines are critical in policy implementation. Politicians seeking immediate results for electoral gains may need more time to establish effective systems. Implementation Analysis assists in developing realistic timelines, especially in creating new organizations requiring staffing and procedural development.

Political Interference Challenges: Political masters, including executives and legislators, may interfere with agency decisions for electoral reasons. Implementation Analysis identifies programmatic arrangements susceptible to political interference and suggests mechanisms to insulate decisions appropriately. The analysis recognizes the challenges of maintaining an "arms-length" relationship to prevent interference, emphasizing the need for careful consideration.

Program Operator Issues: Program operators, delivering services to clients, may deviate from program objectives due to varying working conditions and job norms. The literature portrays operators as saints, shirkers, subverters, shackled, and rent-seekers, reflecting diverse working conditions and risk factors. Implementation Analysis identifies potential issues with front-line workers, recommending clear guidelines, aligned goals, and performance monitoring to mitigate "unsaintly" behavior.

A thorough Implementation Analysis addresses these challenges systematically, guiding policymakers toward effective policy implementation and better outcomes.

Target Compliance Challenges in Policy Implementation

Even when resource constraints and front-line worker behavior are managed, government policies' intended "targets" may not behave as anticipated. This non-compliance can stem from various sources, demanding distinct strategic responses. The primary challenges include insufficient incentives, behavioral biases highlighted by behavioral economics, poor monitoring and enforcement of incentive structures, information gaps, and target hostility or distrust.

Insufficient Incentives: Targets may only comply with adequate incentives. For instance, workers may need to make choices in a pension system with a perceived satisfactory default option. Compliance costs, such as bureaucratic hassles for means-tested benefits, can deter adherence. A well-designed incentive structure may only succeed if well monitored and enforced.

Behavioral Economics Insights: Behavioral economics recognizes individuals as often ill-informed and inclined to follow the path of least resistance. Even with a well-designed incentive structure, compliance may only succeed if aligned with behavioral tendencies. Loss aversion, sensitivity to others' opinions, and herd mentality influence behavior. Effective Implementation Analysis must consider these behavioral aspects for targeted outcomes.

Information Gaps and Hostility: Targets may need more essential information, human capital, or resources, hindering compliance. For instance, low-income individuals may not purchase subsidized health insurance due to resource constraints. Hostility or lack of trust in the government can also contribute to non-compliance.

Strategic Responses: Each barrier to target compliance demands tailored responses. Addressing information shortages and inertia requires providing targets with more information and simplifying choice sets. Adjusting incentives, monitoring, and enforcement are crucial. Implementation Analysis, identifying potential non-compliance sources, aids in devising effective strategies.

A Framework for Implementation Analysis

Step 1: Analyze Implementation Tasks: Identify specific tasks required by a reform proposal, especially when details are lacking. For complex proposals, merely listing key tasks can be a substantial undertaking.

Step 2: Compare with Analysis Checklist: Compare proposed legislation with the Implementation Analysis checklist, prioritizing likely sources of implementation failure using the "warning signs" screening device in Table 1.

Step 3: Gather Preliminary Evidence: Collect initial evidence on potential implementation challenges and barriers to successful implementation for a specific policy proposal.

Step 4: Conduct Detailed Analysis: Analyze key risks, gathering evidence on how challenges may manifest in practice, involving various forms of evidence and skill sets based on the implementation task.

Step 5: Publish Report: A comprehensive report on key implementation risks provides options for changes. The report draws on potential strategic responses, avoiding a one-size-fits-all recommendation and allowing Congress flexibility in decision-making.

Key Considerations for Implementation Analysis

Analytical Issues in Implementation Analysis: Implementation Analysis faces analytical and political challenges, requiring careful consideration of institutional homes, task identification, resource availability, and potential unknowns.

Organizational Overload Concerns: A pilot program with a sunset provision can be implemented to prevent organizational overload. Congressional leaders can designate bills for Implementation Analysis, ensuring their targeted and impactful use.

Timeline Issues: Addressing potential timeline concerns involves implementing a two- or three-year lead time before the first analysis, allowing the implementing organization to build capacity, develop methodologies, and minimize short-term political and policy costs.

An effective Implementation Analysis provides valuable insights into policy challenges, aiding policymakers in creating more successful and well-informed reform proposals.

Political Hurdles and Prospects for Implementation Analysis

Despite the potential benefits of Implementation Analysis, it faces significant political hurdles that have hindered its widespread adoption. Politicians prioritize receiving credit for passed legislation rather than addressing potential implementation issues. The responsibility for implementation is often seen as belonging to others, excluding potential implementing agencies from significant involvement in legislative development. Additionally, majority parties in Congress may view Implementation Analysis as a hindrance to their policy proposals, creating a reluctance to embrace the practice.

Political Interests and Intrigues: The reluctance of majority parties to support Implementation Analysis is rooted in their preference for smooth policy enactment without additional hurdles. In contrast, minority parties find value in using Implementation Analysis to challenge and obstruct majority-party initiatives. This political dynamic hampers the widespread acceptance of Implementation Analysis, as those with the power to enact it often need more incentive.

Potential Solutions: Addressing the barriers to Implementation Analysis requires strategic solutions. A trial run of Implementation Analysis, with a limited number of analyses per year, could be initiated and subject to reauthorization after four years. The Government Accountability Office (GAO) should be designated as the implementing agency. This phased approach allows for simultaneous methodology refinement over the trial period, adapting to challenges and improving the analysis process.

Balancing Delay and Quality: Critics argue that requiring Implementation Analysis for every policy proposal may introduce further conservative bias and hinder policy changes. However, proponents contend that the potential delay is justified to prevent flawed legislation and garner public support. A GAO Implementation Analysis "seal of approval" could enhance a proposal's chances for enactment, balancing the trade-off between delay and quality.

Politicization Concerns: The potential politicization of Implementation Analysis and the associated agency is a valid concern. However, drawing from the Congressional Budget Office's experience, it is feasible to manage the risk of politicization. The CBO has maintained objectivity in its analyses, even with impactful scorecards.

Sensitivity to Political Interference: Recognizing the sensitivity of issues related to political interference, early iterations of Implementation Analysis may need to tread carefully. While potential interference problems can be acknowledged, an in-depth analysis might be deferred to ensure the initial success of the procedure.

In sum, Implementation Analysis holds promise but should be introduced gradually on a trial basis, allowing for adjustments and refinements. With a limited number of analyses per year and a sunset provision after four years, the Government Accountability Office can spearhead this effort. While not a cure-all, Implementation Analysis emerges as a potent tool to enhance informed decision-making and ensure that government policies align with their intended objectives.

Review Questions

1. How does Implementation Analysis address ambiguities in legislation, and why must legislators identify and resolve them?
2. What role do organizational culture and mission play in the potential conflicts identified by Implementation Analysis, and how can policy-makers decide whether to create new implementing agencies or adapt existing ones?
3. How does Implementation Analysis contribute to better government performance, especially in addressing resource and organizational capacity constraints?
4. What are the primary challenges in achieving target compliance in policy implementation, and how does Implementation Analysis propose distinct strategic responses for each challenge?
5. Describe the step-by-step process of Implementation Analysis, highlighting its key components and the role of the GAO in the analysis.
6. Why does Implementation Analysis face political hurdles, and what

strategic solutions are proposed to overcome these barriers?

Discussion Points

1. Balancing Timeliness and Thoroughness in Implementation Analysis: Discuss the potential trade-off between conducting a thorough Implementation Analysis and the need for timely policy enactment. How can policymakers strike a balance to ensure both the quality of analysis and the expeditious implementation of policies?

2. Ensuring Non-Politicization of Implementation Analysis: Explore ways to ensure that Implementation Analysis remains objective and non-politicized. Drawing from the experience of the Congressional Budget Office, discuss strategies to manage the risk of politicization in the analysis process.

3. Public Awareness and Support for Implementation Analysis: How can policymakers enhance public awareness of the benefits of Implementation Analysis? Discuss strategies for garnering public support for this approach and how a GAO "seal of approval" might contribute to its acceptance.

CHAPTER EIGHT: FISCAL SCRUTINY: CASE STUDIES OF FISCAL COUNCILS AND INDEPENDENT BUDGET OFFICES

Summary of Key Points

1. Belgium – High Council of Finance (HCF): Upholding and Building Credibility

- Established in the 1930s, the HCF in Belgium evolved to focus on fiscal discipline and recommendations on borrowing requirements.
- Though formally advisory, the HCF gained a reputation for independent analysis, facing occasional challenges to its independence.
- Functions include advising on fiscal policies and normative recommendations, monitoring regional fiscal policies, and assessing Euro convergence.
- Media presence is crucial for indirect influence, and the HCF's impact varied over pre- and post-euro adoption periods.

2. Canada – Parliamentary Budget Officer (PBO): Navigating Early Challenges for Credibility

- The PBO, established in 2006, aimed to enhance government accountability, transparency, and ethical standards.
- Despite initial uncertainties, the PBO gained credibility through independent expertise, challenging fiscal forecasts, and effective media

engagement.

- Functions include economic analysis, fiscal forecasts, costing proposals, and active participation in public discourse.
- The PBO's media presence, led by Kevin Page, contributed to its growing credibility and influence despite disputes with the government.

3. Hungary – Fiscal Council Evolution: Navigating Political Changes

- The Hungarian Fiscal Council, established in 2008, faced political tensions, leading to significant reforms in 2010.
- Originally with a comprehensive mandate, reforms limited its focus to assessing the state budget, facing challenges to independence.
- Media engagement was initially strong but declined during the reform period, and lessons learned include challenges in polarized political landscapes.

4. Korea's National Assembly Budget Office (NABO)

- Established in 2003, NABO aimed to provide impartial fiscal expertise to Parliament during a period of divided government.
- Functions include analyzing national finances, offering alternative forecasts, costing proposals, and contributing to legislative activities.
- Despite concerns about director appointments, NABO played a crucial role during economic shifts, contributing to improved fiscal accuracy.

5. The Netherlands' Bureau for Economic Policy Analysis (CPB): A Well-Established and Respected Institution

- Founded in 1945, CPB operates within the Ministry of Economic Affairs but maintains operational and analytical independence.
- CPB's extensive mandate covers economic forecasts, cost-benefit analyses, and policy evaluations, influencing policy discussions.
- Media coverage, strategic report releases, and consistent visibility con-

tribute to CPB's credibility and impact in the Netherlands.

6. Sweden's Fiscal Policy Council: Addressing Institutional Gaps with Resource Constraints

- Established in 2007 during fiscal stability, the FPC aimed to enhance long-term fiscal sustainability and provide independent evaluations.
- The FPC's functions include reviewing government fiscal policies and contributing to public debate despite limited resources.
- Media engagement is crucial for the FPC's effectiveness, and despite challenges, it has influenced fiscal policy and maintained independence.

7. United States Congressional Budget Office (CBO): A Guiding Model for Emerging Fiscal Councils

- Established in 1974, the CBO provides objective and impartial information to Congress, operating independently within the legislative branch.
- Functions cover alternative forecasts, analyses of fiscal policies, costing of legislative proposals, and aiding Congress in budget resolutions.
- The CBO's success lies in its credibility, nonpartisan fiscal analysis, and influential role in costing legislative proposals, setting an example for emerging fiscal councils.

Belgium – High Council of Finance (HCF): Upholding and Building Credibility

Belgium features multiple independent fiscal bodies in its budget process. The High Council of Finance (HCF), established in the 1930s, plays a pivotal role. Over time, reforms, especially in 1989, reshaped the HCF's role to focus on promoting fiscal discipline and issuing recommendations on borrowing requirements. Challenges such as high budget deficits and public debt prompted these changes. The Maastricht criteria and Euro commitment further expanded the HCF's normative role to include monitoring compliance with the Stability and Growth Pact (SGP).

Formally advisory to the finance ministry and not legally independent, the HCF has gained a reputation for independent analysis. The Council, comprising a chair, two deputy chairs, and 24 members, is appointed for renewable five-year terms. Membership balance spans expertise, regional and linguistic diversity, and political affiliations. Divided into two sections and supported by a secretariat, the HCF faces occasional challenges to its independence, notably in the mid-2000s when consensus on the Public Sector Borrowing Requirement (PSBR) composition delayed fiscal recommendations.

Functions: The HCF's mandate is to advise the Minister of Finance and Budget on fiscal, financial, and budgetary policy. It produces normative recommendations, monitors regional fiscal policies, formulates medium-term financial objectives, and assesses Euro convergence. Unlike the Federal Planning Bureau (FPB), the HCF does not engage in macroeconomic forecasts or cost political proposals.

Analysis and Impact: The HCF's performance is divided into pre- and post-euro adoption periods. Pre-euro, convergence criteria alignment led to substantial influence and followed recommendations, resulting in positive fiscal outcomes. Post-euro adoption, the decline in convergence criteria influence saw eroding appeal and a deteriorating primary balance due to deviations from recommendations. Notable episodes include the early years of euro adoption aligning with recommendations, critical assessments in 2004, and a lack of reports in 2005-2006. During deviations from fiscal targets, the HCF aims to raise alarms, heavily relying on media presence for indirect influence.

Media Presence Importance: Ensuring a robust media presence is crucial for the High Council of Finance (HCF) to convey its messages effectively. During the lead-up to and initial stages of euro adoption, the HCF garnered substantial press coverage in Belgium. However, this visibility declined over the 2000s, corresponding with a diminishing influence of the Council. Notably, in 2004, when the HCF openly criticized government policies, media reports surged. Conversely, the HCF's media footprint substantially reduced during the period without a formal chair for the PSBR group, despite emerging discrepancies in 2006.

Influence and Reception: While the HCF initially raised alarms, it gained significant attention only when it adopted a more critical stance. Media and government responsiveness followed stronger normative statements against government policies. However, the subsequent two-year vacancies in the PSBR group, during which no recommendations were given, underscored the HCF's operational independence limitations. This pause was successful in diminishing its operational capacity and media presence. Over the last two decades, the HCF's impact on fiscal policy has varied. The division of responsibilities between the HCF and the Federal Planning Bureau theoretically allows for technical specialization and reduced political pressure. Despite criticism for lacking legal and operational independence and being chaired by the Minister of Finance, the HCF's influence was more pronounced in the pre-euro period when consensus existed.

Canada – Parliamentary Budget Officer (PBO): Navigating Early Challenges for Credibility

In 2006, the Canadian Conservative Party established the Parliamentary Budget Officer (PBO) under the Federal Accountability Act, aiming for governance reforms. This move sought to enhance government accountability, transparency, and ethical standards. The PBO's dual purpose was to furnish parliamentarians with independent expertise for effective oversight and to offer an unbiased evaluation of the Department of Finance's fiscal forecasts, addressing historical accuracy concerns. Commencing operations in 2008, the PBO operates under the Library of Parliament, serving a once-renewable 5-year term. Despite initial uncertainties regarding its legal and operational design, the PBO, led by the first appointee, Kevin Page, gradually found its footing. Challenges arose concerning its location, budget, and mandate, with disputes over reporting structures and tensions arising over the publication of reports. These issues underscored concerns about the PBO's operational independence.

Functions: Modelled after the U.S. Congressional Budget Office, the PBO covers a broad spectrum, including economic analysis, fiscal forecasts, costing of proposals, and the publication of research papers. Operating in a parliamentary system, the PBO addresses the challenge of managing extensive costing requests by prioritizing projects based on materiality and contribution potential. Additionally, it ensures credibility through external expert peer reviews and collaborations with various institutions.

Analysis and Impact: Despite controversies, the PBO has gained a strong reputation domestically and internationally. Emphasizing transparency, the PBO publishes all reports and letters on its website, holds regular press conferences, and actively engages with the media and parliamentary committees. Notably, the PBO has effectively raised alarms on fiscal issues, contributing to public awareness and discussions. Its role in improving the accuracy of government forecasts is evident, as government estimates have become more accurate and less pessimistic since the creation of the PBO. Though contentious, the PBO's costing activity has received significant media attention, contributing to political and public debates on various programs. In sum, the PBO has navigated its critical early years, overcoming challenges to establish itself as a credible and influential entity in Canada's fiscal landscape.

Media Presence: Since its inception, the PBO and its work have garnered significant media attention. Despite lacking a designated press officer, the PBO endeavors to make its work accessible to the media. The absence of a press officer is compensated by efforts to train the media in comprehending and utilizing PBO reports. Kevin Page, the inaugural PBO, serves as the public face of the office, earning him the moniker "budget watchdog." Figure 4 illustrates the gradual increase in media coverage, reflecting the Council's growing credibility and reputation.

Challenges and Disputes: During the final six months of Kevin Page's term, media focus intensified as the PBO engaged in a court battle with the government over its mandate. Disagreements arose, with government ministers accusing Page of exceeding his mandate, while he criticized the government for neglecting the successor appointment process and undermining the office's independence.

The PBO's commitment to delivering high-quality, independent analysis through research, costings, and forecasting has solidified its reputation. The strategy of actively engaging with fiscal policy issues, transparent reporting, and media outreach has elevated the Council's profile and influence. However, this proactive stance has also led to clashes with the government, prompting legal interventions to clarify institutional setup and independence issues.

Individual vs. Collective Leadership: Opting for a Parliamentary Budget Officer instead of a multi-member council provides a clear public face but risks associating the Council's identity solely with one individual. The transition to a new PBO becomes crucial, influencing the Council's enduring impact. To maintain independence, the outgoing PBO suggests institutional changes, such as parliamentary appointment and independent office status.

Hungary – Fiscal Council Evolution: Navigating Political Changes

Amid the 2007 Hungarian elections, fiscal concerns took center stage, leading to the enactment of the Fiscal Responsibility Law in November 2008. This legislation established a fiscal council to reform Hungary's fiscal policy framework and enhance transparency. The original fiscal council design included three non-partisan members with a broad mandate, complemented by a technical staff. The Council monitored compliance with fiscal rules and provided independent assessments. However, tensions with the government led to significant revisions in 2010, resulting in a reduced and more compliant model. The reformed Council, with a chairman appointed by the President, central bank governor, and state audit office head, faced funding cuts and a narrower mandate.

Functions Over Two Periods: Initially, the Council had a comprehensive mandate covering macro-fiscal scenarios, costings, and compliance monitoring. After reforms, its focus shifted primarily to assessing the state budget and supporting Parliament's legislative activities, with limitations on forecasting and cost assessments.

Challenges and Controversies: Tensions between the government and the Council, particularly over criticisms of economic policies, led to the 2010 reform. Despite the official rationale being budgetary savings, some argue it aimed at reducing the Council's influence. The restructured Council retained the power to veto budget laws but with limited resources.

Hungary's fiscal Council underwent a significant transformation, adapting to political changes while facing challenges to its independence and influence. The evolution reflects the delicate balance between fiscal oversight and government dynamics.

Media Engagement: Hungary's Fiscal Council, an independent state institution formed by parliamentary legislation, aimed to provide timely assessments of the budgetary implications of government and parliamentary decisions, making this information widely accessible. The Council actively employed the media to disseminate its message. Initial interest during the establishment phase increased when the Council became operational in 2009 and 2010. However, late 2010 and 2011, media reports primarily focused on the Council's reform. Despite facing widespread protests from international and domestic press and criticism from professional and academic circles, the Council underwent reform and budget cuts. The international press, including The Wall Street Journal in November 2010, reported on the dissolution of the Fiscal Council and the creation of a new committee with a more limited composition.

Lessons Learned: Hungary's experience underscores fiscal councils' challenges in highly polarized political landscapes. Balancing the watchdog role, often involving government criticism, with protecting independence is a delicate task. The failure of Hungary's Council to fully launch emphasizes the importance of building institutional credibility and trust, acknowledging that these attributes are only automatically understood or recognized with tangible proof over the long term.

Korea's National Assembly Budget Office (NABO)

In 2003, the Korean National Assembly Budget Office (NABO) was established as an independent entity driven by political considerations within a broader democratic reform agenda. During a period of divided government, NABO aimed to provide Parliament with impartial fiscal expertise, enabling effective scrutiny of the President's budget proposals. Despite stable public finances at the time, the NABO addressed the need for balanced information and capacity to assess draft budgets. Regulated by the National Assembly Budget Office Act, NABO is exclusively accountable to the National Assembly. The Director, appointed by the Speaker based on expert recommendations, serves at the Speaker's discretion. The Director's potential dismissal, overseen by the House Steering Committee, introduces a discussion point in the conclusions. External advisors, comprising experts in public finance, provide additional guidance.

Functions: Modeled after the U.S. Congressional Budget Office (CBO), NABO supports legislative activities by analyzing national finances and policies. Operating with principles of independence, non-partisanship, expertise, and credibility, NABO undertakes essential functions such as monitoring fiscal policy, providing alternative forecasts, costing proposals, and conducting evaluations. Unlike other fiscal councils, NABO uniquely focuses on project and policy assessments, offering recommendations for operational improvements.

Analysis and Impact: Despite robust public finances initially, NABO played a crucial role during economic shifts. Noteworthy instances include warning about expenditure increases, providing conservative fiscal forecasts, and scrutinizing budget drafts. The media's coverage of NABO evolved from low resonance initially to increased attention over the years, mirroring the council's growing reputation.

Over a decade, NABO matured into a vital institution, enhancing transparency in government budgetary data. While considered a conservative and sensible voice in public discussions, NABO's independence, mandated by law, remains intact. However, the absence of a fixed term limit for the Director raises concerns about potential political influence, as directors tend to resign when House Speakers change. Despite this, NABO contributes significantly to fiscal policy discussions and alternative forecasts, demonstrating its impact on Korea's democratic system.

The Netherlands' Bureau for Economic Policy Analysis (CPB): A Well-Established and Respected Institution

Founded in 1945, post-World War II, the Netherlands' Bureau for Economic Policy Analysis (CPB) is distinguished among fiscal councils. Initially created as a planning agency, Jan Tinbergen, a Nobel Prize-winning economist, shaped its trajectory, emphasizing independent analysis. Over the years, CPB expanded its roles, providing economic forecasts, evaluating public finances, and conducting various analyses, contributing significantly to the nation's economic planning. Formally a branch of the civil service under the Ministry of Economic Affairs (MEA), CPB is funded by the MEA but can receive up to twenty per cent of its budget from external assignments, ensuring a degree of financial independence. The Director, appointed for a seven-year term, is selected by the Minister, with an understanding that the appointee is a respected economist and nonpartisan. Despite being financially dependent on the MEA, CPB maintains operational and analytical independence, supported by a supervisory committee and regular independent evaluations.

Functions: CPB's extensive mandate encompasses key fiscal council functions, from providing macroeconomic forecasts for the budget to conducting cost-benefit analyses and evaluating policy proposals. Although it does not directly influence fiscal policy, CPB informs the government and Parliament regarding adherence to coalition agreements. Notably, its role in costing electoral platforms has influenced the quality of public information and shaped policy discussions.

Analysis and Impact: CPB has gained considerable public credibility over its history, contributing to the Netherlands' sound fiscal performance. While the specific impact of CPB's contributions is challenging to isolate, the country's fiscal outcomes over the past 15 years have been notably sound. CPB's forecasts show minimal bias and compliance with fiscal targets has been largely satisfactory. The council actively engages during critical fiscal episodes, signaling deviations from agreed deficit ceilings.

Media Coverage: CPB's media visibility aligns with strategic report releases in March and September, contributing to the public debate. While establishing a causal link between CPB activities and improved fiscal performance is challenging, its consistent media presence contributes to quality public discourse and reduces information asymmetries.

In contrast to other fiscal councils emphasizing independence, CPB operates within the budget process, fostering close collaboration with government ministries. Its avoidance of normative language and policy advice bolsters its impartial image, focusing on providing economic arguments rather than interfering with political debates. CPB's successful integration into the budgetary and political processes demonstrates that a council can maintain independence, contribute effectively, and sustain a visible media presence.

Sweden's Fiscal Policy Council: Addressing Institutional Gaps with Resource Constraints

In a departure from fiscal councils formed during crises, Sweden's Fiscal Policy Council (FPC) emerged in a period of stable public finances. Established in 2007 by a liberal-conservative government, the FPC aimed to enhance long-term fiscal sustainability and provide room for counter-cyclical measures during economic downturns. While complementing existing fiscal frameworks, such as the surplus rule and expenditure ceiling, the FPC filled a specific institutional gap, focusing on an independent evaluation of the Swedish government's fiscal policy. Formally designated a government agency, the FPC operates under the 2007 Ordinance, which was later revised in 2011. Comprising five part-time members and a small secretariat, the council faces budget constraints, with funds included in the Ministry of Finance's annual budget. Members appointed by the government based on council proposals serve fixed terms, ensuring a balance of expertise, practical experience, and gender representation. While directly accountable to the Ministry of Finance, the FPC maintains a close relationship with the Parliament's Finance Committee.

Functions: The FPC's broad mandate centres on reviewing and monitoring tasks, distinct from producing forecasts or costing policies. It evaluates the government's fiscal policy objectives, including the surplus rule and expenditure ceiling, assessing their alignment with cyclical economic developments and long-term sustainable growth. Despite lacking a formal role in the budget process, the council actively contributes to public debate on economic policies.

Analysis and Impact: Established during a period of fiscal stability, the FPC provided both favorable and critical assessments of the government's fiscal policies. Beyond rule compliance, the council delves into sophisticated issues, emphasizing fair intergenerational distribution, tax efficiency, and building precautionary buffers. Notably, during the 2009 economic crisis, the FPC recommended a stronger fiscal stimulus, deviating from traditional expectations and aligning with its mandate. Despite initial concerns from opposition parties, the FPC's reports have proven crucial in critiquing various aspects of government policies, influencing opposition parties in developing their economic policies. While the council does not produce forecasts, its reviews of government forecasts have contributed to a shift from pessimistic to minor optimistic errors.

In a short period, the FPC has established independence and gained reputational capital through normative analysis and an active role in criticizing the government when necessary. However, tensions with the Ministry of Finance have surfaced due to critical comments, highlighting the challenge of sustaining its role with limited resources.

Media Coverage: Given its indirect influence and absence of a formal role in the budget process, media engagement is crucial for the FPC's effectiveness. Over time, the council has successfully increased media coverage, positioning itself as a reliable source for independent economic analysis. Regular reports and interviews with FPC members contribute to its visibility and influence.

Despite resource limitations and lack of budgetary independence, the FPC has influenced fiscal policy in Sweden. Its strategy of establishing independence through normative analysis and active communication has proven successful, aided by political and public consensus on fiscal sustainability. The challenge lies in maintaining its watchdog role within the existing institutional framework and with constrained resources.

United States Congressional Budget Office (CBO): A Guiding Model for Emerging Fiscal Councils

Established in 1974 amid heightened political tensions between Congress and President Richard Nixon over the budget, the Congressional Budget Office (CBO) arose from the Congressional Budget and Impoundment Control Act. This legislative act aimed to reassert Congress' authority in the budget process, shifting the balance from presidential dominance. The CBO's primary role is to provide Congress with objective and impartial information about budgetary and economic issues. Operating independently within the legislative branch, it began operations in February 1975.

As the largest fiscal council with a staff of around 240 in 2012, the CBO operates independently from the President and is not directly affiliated with any Congressional Committee. Its funding is part of the legislative branch budget, and the Director is appointed by the Speaker of the House and the President pro-tempore of the Senate, ensuring a four-year fixed term with the possibility of renewal. Despite theoretical non-partisanship, some Directors had political affiliations before the appointment, operating impartially once in office. With a predominantly Ph.D.-qualified staff in economics, the CBO maintains a nonpartisan reputation through transparent reporting of assumptions and methodologies in its analyses.

Functions: The CBO's extensive mandate covers various fiscal council functions. It produces alternative forecasts, reviews government forecasts, conducts independent analyses of fiscal policies, and provides costings of legislative proposals. Preparing baseline budget projections, economic forecasts, and fiscal sustainability reports for up to 75 years, the CBO aids Congress in developing budget resolutions. It engages in monthly analyses of federal spending and revenue, evaluates specific federal programs, and examines challenges in policy fields like health care, education, taxes, and more. The CBO is crucial in scoring legislation against budget baselines and established fiscal rules.

Analysis and Impact: Forecast Accuracy: While the CBO indirectly influences the accuracy of governmental forecasts by comparing its forecasts with those of the Office of Management and Budget (OMB), evidence shows no consistent bias in the government's revenue forecasts. Post-CBO establishment, average forecast errors remained low, suggesting the CBO's role as a preventative agent against deliberately optimistic revenue forecasts.

Fiscal Activity: Analyzing media activity against fiscal events, the CBO has been active during periods of fiscal policy changes. However, during intense policymaking periods, like the 2001 Bush-era tax cuts, media activity did not noticeably increase, possibly due to a lack of agreed fiscal benchmarks. The CBO's effectiveness shines in its costing role, influencing policy debates by providing independent analyses. It has successfully navigated politically charged environments, offering objective insights into proposed legislation.

Media Coverage: With a significantly increased media presence, the CBO strategically times interventions to align with budget and economic outlook updates. Media coverage reflects the value placed on the CBO's independent analysis.

The CBO stands out as a successful fiscal council, setting an example for others. Its credibility, nonpartisan fiscal analysis, and influential role in costing legislative proposals contribute to its effectiveness. Despite challenges in influencing politicians and the public to constrain deficit increases, the CBO remains a role model. Its success is context-specific, emphasizing the need for new fiscal councils to adapt models to their institutional and political environments.

Review Questions

1. How did the HCF in Belgium adapt to changing fiscal challenges and expand its normative role over time?

2. What were the initial challenges faced by the PBO in Canada, and how did it establish credibility in the fiscal landscape?

3. What lessons can be learned from the evolution of Hungary's Fiscal Council, especially regarding the impact of political changes on its mandate and independence?

4. In what ways did NABO in Korea contribute to improved fiscal accuracy, and how did it navigate challenges related to director appointments?

5. How does the CPB in the Netherlands balance its role within the Ministry of Economic Affairs while maintaining operational and analytical independence?

6. What challenges did the FPC in Sweden face in addressing institutional gaps with limited resources, and how did it contribute to fiscal policy discussions?

7. What makes the CBO in the United States a guiding model for emerging fiscal councils, and how does its structure contribute to its success?

Discussion Points

1. Media Influence on Fiscal Councils: Discuss the importance of media presence for fiscal councils in influencing public perception, political decisions, and overall effectiveness. How can fiscal councils strategically engage with the media to enhance their impact?

2. Operational Independence vs. Budget Constraints: Explore the tension between maintaining operational independence and dealing with budget constraints for fiscal councils. How can fiscal councils navigate limited resources while ensuring their effectiveness and credibility?

3. Political Dynamics and Fiscal Council Evolution: Analyze how the political landscape influences the evolution of fiscal councils. What challenges do fiscal councils face in maintaining independence and relevance amid political changes?

CONCLUSION

The book "FISCAL POLITICS INTRIGUES: MANAGING COVID-19 CRISIS AND BUDGET SCRUTINY STRATEGIES," explores fiscal intricacies, crisis management, and budget scrutiny in the face of unprecedented challenges. The book reveals a profound tapestry of interconnected global economic forces, political dynamics, and the institutional frameworks that underpin fiscal decision-making. Chapter One highlighted the government's crucial role in shaping economic paths through fiscal policies and traced the evolution of fiscal policy from the pre-Keynesian era to the contemporary challenges posed by digital transactions, Base Erosion and Profit Shifting (BEPS), and the imperative for sustainable green fiscal policies.

Chapter Two delved into the collaborative world of economic policies, emphasizing the distinctions between fiscal and monetary measures. It illuminated the tools governments employed to steer economies and underscored the critical importance of timely, targeted, and temporary stimulus measures, particularly in the aftermath of the 2007-2008 Great Recession. As we turned our attention to the impact of the COVID-19 pandemic in Chapter Three, the dual challenges of health and economic crises unfolded. The chapter presented a nuanced analysis of the four phases of policy response, offering insights into the measures supporting businesses, households, and the broader investment and consumption landscape.

Chapter Four broadened the scope to global perspectives, exploring tax policies and resilience-building strategies for a speedy recovery from the pandemic. It scrutinized liquidity management, social protection systems, tax administration efficiency, stimulus measures, and the anticipated revenue impacts, emphasizing the need for innovative financing and effective domestic resource mobilization. The lens then focused on the Eurozone in Chapter Five, where the spectre of high inflation and external shocks demanded a delicate fiscal dance. The chapter uncovered the intricacies of managing public finances in the face of inflation dynamics, fiscal policy responses, and the distributional impacts on households across income spectrums.

In Chapter Six, we delved into the profound effects of inflation, exploring its distributive effects, impact on households, and the crucial role of fiscal policy in managing inflation. The chapter endorsed endogenous growth theory and highlighted the equity implications of fiscal reforms, recognizing the inherently political nature of fiscal policymaking. Chapter Seven introduced us to the critical concept of Implementation Analysis, advocating for a structured approach to address implementation issues in government programs. It underscored the need for sustained attention, standardized methodologies, and strategic responses to ensure better government performance and the achievement of policy objectives.

Finally, Chapter Eight scrutinized fiscal councils and independent budget offices through case studies from around the world. From Belgium to the United States, these institutions provided lessons in upholding credibility, navigating political changes, addressing resource constraints, and setting guiding examples for emerging fiscal councils.

As we conclude our journey through "FISCAL POLITICS INTRIGUES," the chapters collectively underscore the complexities inherent in fiscal decision-making, the agility required in crisis management, and the pivotal role of robust budget scrutiny mechanisms. In an era marked by unprecedented challenges, the book serves as a compass, guiding policymakers, scholars, and global citizens through the intricacies of fiscal politics, crisis management, and the scrutiny ensuring economic systems' resilience and sustainability.

SOURCES

SOURCES

Fiscal Policy for Economic Development: An Overview Benedict Clements, Sanjeev Gupta, And Gabriela Inchauste https://www.imf.org/external/pubs/nft/2004/hcd/ch01.pdf

Chapter 23 - Environmental Taxation and Regulation A. Lans Bovenberg, Lawrence H. Goulder https://www.sciencedirect.com/science/article/abs/pii/S1573442002800271

Chapter 32 - What is a Sustainable Public Debt? P. D'Erasmo E.G. Mendoza J. Zhang https://www.sciencedirect.com/science/article/abs/pii/S1574004816000148

All About Fiscal Policy: What It Is, Why It Matters, and Examples https://www.investopedia.com/terms/f/fiscalpolicy.asp

"Fiscal Policy" Before Keynes' General Theory Marianne Johnson file:///C:/Users/USER/Downloads/SSRN-id3252526.pdf

Fiscal Policy: Taking and Giving Away Mark Horton, Asmaa El-Ganainy https://www.imf.org/en/Publications/fandd/issues/Series/Back-to-Basics/Fiscal-Policy

Expansionary and Contractionary Fiscal Policy https://courses.lumenlearning.com/wm-macroeconomics/chapter/expansionary-and-contractionary-fiscal-policy/

Expansionary Fiscal Policy: Risks and Examples https://www.investopedia.com/terms/e/expansionary_policy.asp

Monetary Policy vs. Fiscal Policy: What's the Difference? https://www.investopedia.com/ask/answers/100314/whats-difference-between-monetary-policy-and-fiscal-policy.asp

How fiscal policy impacts business https://gocardless.com/guides/posts/how-fiscal-policy-impacts-business/

Fiscal Policy: Economic Effects Jeffrey M. Stupak Analyst in Macroeconomic Policy file:///C:/Users/USER/Documents/public%20finance/201905164572pdf

Tax and Fiscal Policy in Response to the Coronavirus Crisis: Strengthening Confidence and Resilience https://read.oecd-ilibrary.org/view/?ref=128_12 8575-06raktcoaa&title=Tax-and-Fiscal-Policy-in-Response-to-the-Coro navirus-Crisis

Fiscal policy and high inflation https://www.ecb.europa.eu/pub/economic-bulletin/articles/2023/html/ecb.ebart202302_01~2bd46eff8f.en.html

All About Fiscal Policy: What It Is, Why It Matters, and Examples ADAM HAYES https://www.investopedia.com/terms/f/fiscalpolicy.asp

A Monetary and Fiscal History of the United States, 1961-2022 alan blinder https://www.milkenreview.org/articles/a-monetary-and-fiscal-history-of -the-united-states-1961-2022

Interactions between fiscal and monetary policies: a brief history of a long relationship https://www.pse-journal.hr/en/archive/interactions-between-fiscal-and-monetary-policies-a-brief-history-of-a-long-relationship_7 902/

Taxation https://www.britannica.com/money/topic/taxation

Chapter 2 Fundamental principles of taxation https://www.oecd-ilibrary .org/docserver/9789264218789-5-en.pdf?e=1703964323&id=id&accname= guest&checksum=91EDD7C1544E5D4777ECE5A320702571

The Theoretical Foundations of Regulation on Public Finances http://real. mtak.hu/146408/1/CEALSCEPhD02RegulationofPublicFinances2.pdf

Public Finance: Theory and Practice in the Central European Transition https://www.nispa.org/files/publications/ebooks/Public-Finance-Theory-and-Practice.pdf

What Are Public Goods? Definition, How They Work, and Example JASON FERNANDO https://www.investopedia.com/terms/p/public-good.asp

Public Goods https://courses.lumenlearning.com/wm-microeconomics/chapter/public-goods/

The rationale for public sector intervention in the economy https://www.london.gov.uk/sites/default/files/gla_migrate_files_destination/rationale_for_public_sector_intervention.pdf

Free Rider Benefiting from a common resource without paying for it https://corporatefinanceinstitute.com/resources/economics/free-rider/

Free-rider problem https://en.wikipedia.org/wiki/Free-rider_problem#:~:text=In%20the%20social%20sciences%2C%20the,goods%20of%20a%20communal%20nature

The advantage of international fiscal cooperation under alternative monetary regimes https://www.sciencedirect.com/science/article/abs/pii/S0176268096000122

Who benefits from international fiscal cooperation? The role of cross-country asymmetries George Liontos a, Apostolis Philippopoulos https://www.sciencedirect.com/science/article/abs/pii/S1703494923000026

International tax cooperation and capital mobility https://repositorio.cepal.org/server/api/core/bitstreams/e4d0935a-6ae8-4ba7-8430-c7601f8cb058/content

Case Studies of Fiscal Councils—Functions and Impact https://www.imf.org/external/np/pp/eng/2013/071613a.pdf

Chapter 7 Broader tax challenges raised by the digital economy https://www.oecd-ilibrary.org/docserver/9789264218789-10-en.pdf?expires=1703975653&id=id&accname=guest&checksum=410D401BCAC2A4DD84E56FC0ED2A1892

Taxing the Digital Economy in Latin America and the Caribbean: What can be done https://www.afronomicslaw.org/2020/12/09/taxing-the-digital-economy-in-latin-america-and-the-caribbean-what-can-be-done

Green Fiscal Reforms, Environment and Sustainable Development https://onlineacademicpress.com/index.php/IJAEFA/article/view/6/375

What Are Smart Contracts on the Blockchain and How They Work https://www.investopedia.com/terms/s/smart-contracts.asp

Aging Populations and
Public Pension Schemes https://www.imf.org/external/pubs/nft/op/147/

Fiscal Policy David N. Weil https://www.econlib.org/library/Enc/FiscalPoli

cy.html

Do Enlarged Fiscal Deficits Cause Inflation: The Historical Record Michael D. Bordo Mickey D. Levy Working Paper 28195 https://www.nber.org/system/files/working_papers/w28195/w28195.pdf

Fiscal Policy Can Help Tame Inflation and Protect the Most Vulnerable https://www.imf.org/en/Blogs/Articles/2023/04/03/fiscal-policy-can-help-tame-inflation-and-protect-the-most-vulnerable

Public Policy Origins, Practice, and Analysis https://web.ung.edu/media/university-press/public-policy.pdf?t=1661449833017

What are the principles of good taxation? https://www.futurelearn.com/info/courses/public-financial-management/0/steps/14705#:~:text=The%20principles%20of%20good%20taxation%20were%20formulated%20many%20years%20ago,%2C%20certainty%2C%20convenience%20and%20efficiency

Principles of Taxation https://taxjustice-and-poverty.org/fileadmin/Dateien/Taxjustice_and_Poverty/Introduction/05_Principles.pdf

Taxes Definition: Type, Who Pays and Why https://www.investopedia.com/terms/t/taxes.asp

Classes of taxes https://www.britannica.com/money/topic/taxation/Classes-of-taxes

Analysis of Assessment Methods of Tax Burden: Theoretical Aspect file:///C:/Users/USER/Downloads/2089-Article%20Text-6378-1-10-20120807.pdf

Tax shift https://en.wikipedia.org/wiki/Tax_shift#:~:text=Tax%20shift%20is%20a%20kind,the%20redistribution%20of%20tax%20burden

Distributional effects https://en.wikipedia.org/wiki/Distributional_effects#:~:text=A%20distributional%20effect%20is%20the,cost%20allocations%20of%20a%20project

Government Spending https://corporatefinanceinstitute.com/resources/economics/government-spending/

Government spending https://en.wikipedia.org/wiki/Government_spending

What Are Some Examples of Debt Instruments? https://www.investopedia.c

om/ask/answers/050515/what-are-some-examples-debt-instruments.asp

What Is a Debt Instrument? Definition, Structure, and Types https://www.investopedia.com/terms/d/debtinstrument.asp

Government Debt Management: Designing Debt Management Strategies https://thedocs.worldbank.org/en/doc/194071527797532524-0340022018/original/GDM1backgroundnotes.pdf

How to design a stimulus package https://cepr.org/voxeu/columns/how-design-stimulus-package

Green stimulus after the 2008 crisis: Learning from successes and failures https://www.iea.org/articles/green-stimulus-after-the-2008-crisis

A Comparison of Selected Stimulus Packages in 2008 and 2020: investing in Renewable Energy, Sustainable Agriculture and Food Security, and Gender Equality and the Empowerment of Women for Structural Economic transformation https://unctad.org/system/files/information-document/osg_2020-12-18_StimulusPackages_en.pdf

The United States' Response to COVID-19: A Case Study of the First Year https://globalhealthsciences.ucsf.edu/sites/globalhealthsciences.ucsf.edu/files/covid-us-case-study.pdf

China's Policy Experience in Responding to Covid-19 Shock https://unctad.org/system/files/official-document/BRI-Project_RP24_en.pdf

The Origins of Greece's Debt Crisis https://www.investopedia.com/articles/personal-finance/061115/origins-greeces-debt-crisis.asp#:~:text=The%20Greek%20debt%20crisis%20is,over%20the%20next%20thirty%20years

The IMF and the Greek Crisis: Myths and Realities

Speech by Poul Thomsen, Director of the European Department of the International Monetary Fund, at the London School of Economics https://www.imf.org/en/News/Articles/2019/10/01/sp093019-The-IMF-and-the-Greek-Crisis-Myths-and-Realities

Chapter 1. Fiscal Politics https://www.elibrary.imf.org/display/book/9781475547900/ch001.xml

Policy Challenges for the Next 50 Years https://www.oecd.org/economy/Policy-challenges-for-the-next-fifty-years.pdf

But Will It Work?: Implementation Analysis to Improve Government

Performance R. Kent Weaver https://www.brookings.edu/wp-content/upl oads/2016/06/02_implementation_analysis_weaver.pdf

Cross-Border Impacts of Fiscal Policy: Still Relevant? file:///C:/User-s/USER/Downloads/c4.pdf

What Is a Tax Treaty Between Countries & How Does It Work? https://www. investopedia.com/terms/t/taxtreaty.asp

Five common challenges with Operational Transfer Pricing https://www.d eloitte.com/global/en/services/tax/perspectives/five-common-challenges-with-operational-transfer-pricing.html

Common Transfer Pricing Issues and How to Rectify Them https://www.vi etnam-briefing.com/news/transfer-pricing-issues.html/

Regional Financial Cooperation https://repositorio.cepal.org/server/api/ core/bitstreams/c5982d1f-ee4a-464d-8e51-d199b48391b3/content

The Coordination of National Fiscal Policies in the Context of Monetary Union https://www.europarl.europa.eu/workingpapers/econ/pdf/e6en_en. pdf

ASEAN-5: Further Harnessing the Benefits of Regional Integration amid Fragmentation Risks file:///C:/Users/USER/Downloads/wpiea2023191-print-pdf.pdf

Base erosion and profit shifting https://en.wikipedia.org/wiki/Base_erosio n_and_profit_shifting#:~:text=Base%20erosion%20and%20profit%20s hifting%20(BEPS)%20refers%20to%20corporate%20tax,the%20higher% 2Dtax%20jurisdictions%20using

Cap and Trade vs Carbon Tax https://earth.org/cap-and-trade-vs-carbon-tax/#:~:text=While%20a%20carbon%20tax%20sets,the%20rise%20of%2 0global%20temperatures.

Which is better: carbon tax or cap-and-trade? https://www.lse.ac.uk/gran thaminstitute/explainers/which-is-better-carbon-tax-or-cap-and-trade/

What are some ways businesses can incentivize sustainable tourism prac-tices? https://www.linkedin.com/advice/1/what-some-ways-businesses-can-incentivize-sustainable

Practical incentives needed to help firms adopt green practices: official https://vietnamlawmagazine.vn/practical-incentives-needed-to-help-firms-adopt-green-practices-official-69852.html

Green Credit Programme of India: Incentivizing Environmental Actions and Paving the Way for a Sustainable Future https://calculuscarbon.com/green-credit-programme-of-india-incentivizing-environmental-actions-and-paving-the-way-for-a-sustainable-future/

Taxing Cryptocurrencies file:///C:/Users/USER/Downloads/wpiea2023144-print-pdf%20(1).pdf

Social impact bond https://en.wikipedia.org/wiki/Social_impact_bond#:~:text=Social%20Impact%20Bonds%20(SIBs)%20are

Social Impact Bond (SIB): Definition, How It Works, and Example https://www.investopedia.com/terms/s/social-impact-bond.asp

Green Bonds And The Emergence Of Sustainable Finance In The Nigerian Capital Market https://tnp.com.ng/insights/green-bonds-and-the-emergence-of-sustainable-finance-in-the-nigerian-capital-market

Green Bond https://corporatefinanceinstitute.com/resources/esg/green-bond/

South Korea postpones 20% tax on crypto gains to 2025 https://www.forbesindia.com/article/crypto-made-easy/south-korea-postpones-20-tax-on-crypto-gains-to-2025/78341/1

The Current State of Crypto Taxation in South Korea https://www.tekedia.com/the-current-state-of-crypto-taxation-in-south-korea/

Enhancing tax transparency with blockchain technology https://punchng.com/enhancing-tax-transparency-with-blockchain-technology/#:~:text=Blockchain%20technology%20has%20the%20potential,reducing%20tax%20evasion%20and%20fraud

How we use data and analytics https://www.ato.gov.au/about-ato/commitments-and-reporting/information-and-privacy/how-we-use-data-and-analytics

Use of Big Data in Tax Administrations https://www.ciat.org/use-of-big-data-in-tax-administrations/?lang=en

Strategic tax management: best practices help ensure competitiveness https://www.dpc.com.br/strategic-tax-management-best-practices-help-ensure-competitiveness/?lang=en

7 Ways to Maximize Tax Savings with Strategic Tax Management https://w
ww.nidhicpa.com/7-ways-to-maximize-tax-savings-with-strategic-tax-
management/

What Are Tax Management Strategies? https://www.trilogyfs.com/tax-
management-strategies/

Corporate Tax Planning and Financial Performance of Development Banks
in Nigeria file:///C:/Users/USER/Downloads/SSRN-id3896368.pdf

Navigating the Nuances: Tax Planning with Legal Precision and Ethical
Integrity https://www.linkedin.com/pulse/navigating-nuances-tax-plann
ing-legal-precision-ethical-fdxec?trk=article-ssr-frontend-pulse_more-
articles_related-content-card

Tax avoidance might be legal but it's time we seriously questioned its ethics
https://www.manchester.ac.uk/discover/news/tax-avoidance-legal-ethics
/

What Are Some Ways to Minimize Tax Liability? https://www.investoped
ia.com/ask/answers/040715/what-are-some-ways-minimize-tax-liability
.asp

6 Strategies to Protect Income from Taxes https://www.investopedia.com/
articles/personal-finance/032116/top-6-strategies-protect-your-income-
taxes.asp

Business Taxation Meaning: Everything You Need to Know https://www
.upcounsel.com/business-taxation-meaning#:~:text=of%20business%20o
perations.-,The%20meaning%20of%20business%20taxation%20refers%
20to%20the%20taxes%20that,for%20adhering%20to%20tax%20regulati
ons

How Does Corporate Taxation Affect Business Investment? Evidence From
Aggregate and Firm-Level Data https://one.oecd.org/document/ECO/WKP(2
023)18/en/pdf

Taxation of Income from Business and Investment https://www.imf.org/exte
rnal/pubs/nft/1998/tlaw/eng/ch16.pdf

The Tax Advantage of Big Business: How the Structure of Corporate Taxation

Fuels Concentration and Inequality https://journals.sagepub.com/doi/10.117 7/0032329220911778

Corporate Tax: Definition, Deductions, How It Works https://www.investo pedia.com/terms/c/corporatetax.asp

Determining the impact of taxation on corporate financial decision-making Savina Princen https://www.cairn.info/revue-reflets-et-perspectives-de- la-vie-economique-2012-3-page-161.htm

Reclaiming corporate tax revenues https://www.epi.org/publication/reclai ming-corporate-tax-revenues/

Tax Planning For Beginners: 6 Key Principles Explained https://www.botk eeper.com/blog/tax-planning-for-beginners-6-key-principles-explained

The Principles of Proactive Tax Planning [Five Considerations for Business Owners] https://warrenaverett.com/insights/the-principles-of-proactive- tax-planning-five-considerations-for-business-owners/

Four Reasons to Align Your Supply Chain and Tax Strategies https://www.b do.com/insights/tax/four-reasons-to-align-your-supply-chain-and-tax- strategies

How do you balance risk and reward in decision making? https://www.link edin.com/advice/0/how-do-you-balance-risk-reward-decision-making

Balancing risk and reward: How C-suite leaders can innovate responsibly https://www.fastcompany.com/90977835/balancing-risk-and-reward-ho w-c-suite-leaders-can-innovate-responsibly

Tax Planning Process https://www.stptax.com/tax-planning/tax-plannin g-process/

What is tax planning? https://www.dsaprospect.co.uk/guides/tax-plannin g

Tax planning process https://taxfitness.com.au/tax-planning/tax-planni ng-process/

4-step process for tax planning https://www.farmprogress.com/manage ment/4-step-process-for-tax-planning

Tax Credit vs. Deduction: What's the Difference? Both reduce your tax bill—but in different ways https://www.wsj.com/buyside/personal-finance/ tax-credit-vs-deduction-6f611898

Tax Deductions & Credits https://www.investopedia.com/tax-deductions-and-credits-4689689

What Is Tax Avoidance and How Is It Different From Tax Evasion? https://www.investopedia.com/terms/t/tax_avoidance.asp

Minimize taxes and maximize your bottom line https://www.investopedia.com/articles/stocks/11/intro-tax-efficient-investing.asp

Tax-Exempt Interest Definition and Examples https://www.investopedia.com/terms/t/taxexemptinterest.asp

Retirement Contribution: Meaning, Types, Limits https://www.investopedia.com/terms/r/retirement-contribution.asp

Tax Break Definition, Different Types, How to Get One https://www.investopedia.com/terms/t/tax-break.asp

How to get the most money back on your tax return https://www.investopedia.com/financial-edge/0312/how-to-get-the-most-money-back-on-your-tax-return.aspx

Tax Credit: What It Is, How It Works, What Qualifies, 3 Types https://www.investopedia.com/terms/t/taxcredit.asp

23 Income Tax Incentives for Investment https://www.imf.org/external/pubs/nft/1998/tlaw/eng/ch23.pdf

Understanding Business Expenses and Which Are Tax Deductible https://www.investopedia.com/terms/b/businessexpenses.asp

Deductible vs. Non-deductible Business Expenses https://www.sorgecpa.com/resources/insights/deductible-vs.-non-deductible-business-expenses

Ordinary and Necessary Expense: What it is, How it Works https://www.investopedia.com/terms/o/oandne.asp

Amortization vs. Depreciation: What's the Difference? https://www.investopedia.com/ask/answers/06/amortizationvsdepreciation.asp#:~:text=Amortization%20and%20depreciation%20are%20two,to%20reflect%20its%20anticipated%20deterioration

Amortization vs. Depreciation: What's the Difference? https://www.investopedia.com/ask/answers/06/amortizationvsdepreciation.asp#:~:text=Amortization%20and%20depreciation%20are%20two,to%20reflect%20its%20anticipated%20deterioration

R&D Tax Credits and Deductions https://pro.bloombergtax.com/brief/rd-tax-credit-and-deducting-rd-expenditures/

Renewable Energy Credits (RECs), Explained https://watchwire.ai/renewable-energy-credits-recs-explained/#:~:text=So%2C%20What%20Exactly%20Are%20Renewable,power%20lines%20that%20transport%20energy.

Navigating the World of Taxation: A Comprehensive Guide https://www.linkedin.com/pulse/navigating-world-taxation-comprehensive-guide#:~:text=Intriguingly%2C%20the%20considerations%20of%20residency,shape%20the%20international%20tax%20landscape

Transfer Pricing: What It Is and How It Works, With Examples https://www.investopedia.com/terms/t/transfer-pricing.asp

International Tax Planning and Compliance https://www.hco.com/insights/international-tax-planning-and-compliance

Guidance Note Compliance Risk Management: Managing and Improving Tax Compliance https://www.oecd.org/tax/administration/33818656.pdf

How Tax Treaties Prevent Tax Leakage in Cross-Border Projects https://www.huntonak.com/en/insights/how-tax-treaties-prevent-tax-leakage-in-cross-border-projects.html

Improving Tax Compliance: Establishing a Risk Management Framework https://www.adb.org/publications/improving-tax-compliance

Internal Audit and Tax Compliance https://myusf.usfca.edu/internal-audit

Internal Control System and Tax Compliance: An Empirical Analysis https://www.ijicc.net/images/vol11iss12/111204_Prawira_2020_E_R.pdf

Navigating Tax Risks in Indirect Tax: A Strategic Guide for Risk Management https://www.complyiq.io/navigating-tax-risks/

The promise and limitations of information technology for tax mobilization https://blogs.worldbank.org/developmenttalk/promise-and-limitations-information-technology-tax-mobilization

Information Technology for Tax Administration https://pdf.usaid.gov/pdf_docs/pnaea485.pdf

5 Tax Planning Examples https://www.modwm.com/5-tax-planning-examples/

4 global tax trends and how they impact your operations https://www.tm f-group.com/en/news-insights/articles/2019/april/global-tax-trend-and-impact-your-operations/

About the Author

Professor Uwem Essia is a distinguished academic and celebrated author known for his illustrious career in leadership, management, economics, and development. Since June 2021, Professor Essia has immersed himself in personal studies and established himself as a prolific online book publisher, with a presence on platforms. He holds a PhD degree in Economics. Professor Uwem Essia's career is a testament to his passion for knowledge, education, and the betterment of society. His vast experience, research contributions, and dedication to fostering positive change make him a prominent figure in leadership, management, and economics. With a wealth of knowledge and a commitment to academic excellence, Professor Essia continues to make a significant impact. He is open to collaboration in joint research work/consulting, Adjunct and remote teaching, theses/dissertation supervision, professorial assessment, article/book editing and previewing, and joint book and article publishing.

You can connect with me on:

🌐 https://digitalgainspro.com

📘 https://www.facebook.com/uwem.essia.3

🔗 https://www.amazon.com/author/uwemessia

Also by Uwem Essia

Fiscal Dynamics in a Transforming Global Economy: Contemporary Issues in Public Finance, the Future of Fiscal Policy, and Projections for 2060

This insightful book delves into the intricate realms of public finance, the evolution of fiscal strategies, and the links between monetary and fiscal policies. Unravel the historical trajectory of fiscal policy schools, navigate the challenges posed by global shifts, and peer into the future of national policies amidst transformative landscapes. From strategic structural reforms fostering sustainable growth to projections for 2060 and beyond, this book provides a nuanced understanding of fiscal intricacies. A must-read for policymakers, economists, and enthusiasts, offering a holistic perspective on navigating the dynamic currents of our ever-evolving global economy. "Fiscal Dynamics in a Transforming Global Economy" is Book 1 of the Series titled "Public Finance, Fiscal Policy and Tax Management."

ECONOMIC GOVERNANCE AND PUBLIC FINANCE DYNAMICS: Public Expenditure Policy and the Path to Sustainable Development

"Economic Governance and Public Finance Dynamics" is the third book of the Series, Public Finance, Fiscal Policy and Tax Management, wherein the author dissects issues of public expenditure policy, public goods, fiscal policies, and fiscal federalism. Each chapter navigates a crucial facet of economic governance linked to fiscal policies' multifaceted nature, exploring the dynamics of debt financing and illuminating the profound impact of public investments on economic development. It offers a comprehensive understanding of economic landscapes, with insights from renowned scholars. The book is a useful intellectual resource for academics and practitioners working on government budget preparation and implementation, economic development planning, and public-private partnerships.

Tax Revenue Optimization, Efficiency, and Strategic Management: From Business Income Tax to International Cooperation

"Tax Revenue Optimization, Efficiency, and Strategic Management." is the second in the Book Series "Public Finance, Fiscal Policy, and Tax Management". This comprehensive guide navigates the complexities of global tax systems, from defining business income and tackling temporal dimensions to unraveling challenges in complex transactions. Explore asset taxation frameworks and finance leases and gain insights into international taxation strategies. The book extends beyond conventional topics, emphasizing collaboration, leadership, and efficient design in transforming tax processes. Budget and tax officials in the public sector, political and business leaders, and academics in the management sciences, economics, and public administration, and those taking professional courses in taxation and accounting will find this book a useful intellectual resource, unlocking the future of tax management in our ever-evolving global economy.